MANAGING

LIFE

WITH KIDS

MANAGING LIFE WITH KIDS

Simple Solutions to Organize
Your Family and Home

Mary Caroline Walker

Booksurge Publishing
7290-B Investment Drive
Charleston, SC 29418

ISBN 1-4196-7504-4
LCCN: 2007906473

Cover design: Steve Lepre/Sunhead Projects, LLC
Photography: Jack Alterman
Typesetting: Fox Meadow Creations

Printed in the United States of America

This book is dedicated to my husband, Joel Walker. Joel was always a constant source of encouragement and helped me create time that I did not have to write this book. I am forever grateful for his positive attitude and always believing in me.

To my four boys who have to live through my various systems until I can get them right; Billy, Jack, Jamie, and Joel Thomas. My love for my boys is what drove me to be as efficient as possible so that I could enjoy the precious time that my husband and I have with them.

And to my father, Douglas M. Heath, from whom I inherited the innate ability to be organized, and to my mother, Mary Seabrook Bradley Heath, who taught me how to have fun and gave me a love for reading, writing, and helping others.

Acknowledgements

I WOULD LIKE TO THANK MY HUSBAND, JOEL WALKER, AND MY four children for their support and without whom I could have never written this book. Their enthusiasm and encouragement kept me focused and driven to write. I am also very thankful for the sacrifices they made to allow me the time it took to complete this book.

For his efforts in helping to make this book a reality, I am forever grateful to my husband, Joel. As I spent my time writing this book, Joel did all of the legwork to help to get it published. Thank you!

Thanks to my mother-in-law, Janet Walker, from whom I learned a lot about keeping an organized home. She also taught me by example, how to entertain gracefully without being stressed.

I would like to thank Lark Sisson McAtee, my cousin and also a mother of four children, whom I always called whenever I faced a parenting predicament with which I needed help. Some of the ideas in this book came from her experience as a mother. I am grateful for Lark always being there with advice and suggestions, and for just being someone I could laugh with when raising four children seemed to be a little too crazy.

Thank you to my older brother Douglas L. Heath, who helped prepare me for life with four boys. He helped me get a better glimpse of insight into the male gender than I ever could have gotten on my own. He also helped to make me a bit tougher, which prepared me for this testosterone-filled house that I manage today.

A Note from the Author

I AM NOT A PERFECT MOTHER, OR HOUSEKEEPER. MY HOUSE is not always free of a mess or without toys all over the floor and I am certainly not June Cleaver! I am, however, a mother of four boys who just wants to enjoy her family more and have realized that by being organized I am better able to do that. I have tried many different routines and systems trying to find the ones that could make my family's life easier and more enjoyable. Not all of them have worked, but I have always been determined to keep trying until I found the ones that did.

As you read through this book, don't think that I'm a mom whose only concern is for everyone to follow her systems to the letter. Yes, I do enforce the systems I have established for my family, but that's only so that after everything is done as it should be, we can all go outside for a good game of baseball or to shoot hoops. When my kids ask me to go outside and play with them while I'm working on something that needs to be done in the house, I quickly remind them that if they help me out, I will be finished sooner and will have more time to play. That usually results in a helping hand or two and shows them that when the work is done, the play can begin. Our family works as a team to accomplish everything in the house so we can play more together.

I love to play! I quickly realized, however, that with each beautiful child my husband and I added to our family I was going to have to become more and more organized so that the time I had to play did not dwindle to nothing. I began taking the approach that I was my family's business manager and needed to be just as organized and use the same managerial skills as I did when I had my career. I began finding out that each system I created allowed me to spend more time playing with my children or visiting with my husband. After that I was addicted! I wanted everything to run smoothly and efficiently to allow myself more time to be a better parent, a better spouse and a better person.

The whole purpose behind organizing your home and your family's life is to be able to enjoy your life to its fullest and create a better environment for your family. Not only will you be helping to take the stress out of your life by implementing the principles in this book, but your family's life will improve because of it. You will be raising your children in a home with order instead of chaos. You will be able to do more with your children and for yourself once you have established routines and systems to help your family's operation run smoothly. I have been fortunate enough to experience the relief from being overwhelmed by parenthood and the benefits of leading an organized life, and I want to share some of what I have learned to help you do the same!

todaysultimate**mom**.com

Free helpful and easy tips to improve yourself and family!

Benefit with up-to-date information that can help you!

➤ Fitness and Diet

➤ Health Issues

➤ Fashion

➤ Entertaining tips

➤ Easy, family-friendly recipes

➤ Educational tips and school-related topics

➤ Cleaning and organization shortcuts

Check out what's happening on

todaysultimate**mom**.com

Table of Contents

todaysultimate**mom**.com

Introduction

NO ONE EVER PLANS TO BE DISORGANIZED OR HAVE THEIR home in a constant state of chaos; it just happens, day by day, paper by paper, pile by pile, until one day you take a step back and wonder "What has happened to my home?" and "How can I ever regain control?"

Everyone thinks they want to be organized, but until you reach the point when you realize that your lack of organization is actually costing you, you will never change your habits. Disorganization costs you in the form of frustration, confusion, cleanliness, and the loss of time spent unnecessarily. This lost time is taken away from your family as well as other events and activities that are important to you.

It is not the single act of being organized that is important, but it is the things that organization gives you. It gives you freedom from being in constant search of your keys, your purse, your child's papers that needed signing, etc. It also gives you a clear brain to think of more important things and free your mind of clutter. Even though being organized takes time and effort, it pays off tenfold in the long run.

Just by reading this book you have come to understand that life can be better if you can just create order in your home. My hope in writing this book is to give you insight and ideas on how to do just that. Being a mother of four boys, all born within five and a half years of each other, has taught me many things, and one of those things is the value of organization. If you apply the principles in this book, you will be able to regain order in your home and have a more fulfilled life by getting rid of the negative effects of disorganization.

1

Regaining Order in Your Home

TRYING TO REGAIN ORDER IN YOUR HOME REQUIRES A GAME plan and time. It does not happen overnight. Think of it like dieting: you do not decide to lose 20 pounds and then suddenly, "poof!" it's gone. You have to set small goals and work at it daily, one step at a time. At first you may see only a little progress, but then suddenly one day you realize that you can slip into that size six dress, just as one day you will find that your home is finally running like a well-oiled machine.

Also, like keeping those lost pounds off, you cannot go back to your old habits. You have to continue to do the things that gave you success in the first place. It becomes easier and easier to develop better habits when you see how your life is changing for the better once you have created order in your home. The things that at first may seem difficult to do will become second nature to you. In fact, you will feel better once you have done the little things that help you to stay organized.

Now that you have made the decision to get organized, you will need to dedicate time to read through this book and apply its principles. Some of the ideas may be more fitting for your family than others. You may try a principle that I have suggested and then tweak it to fit the needs of your family. All of the principles that I have mentioned in this book have helped make my life in a family of six a lot easier. Remember that it is not just one of the concepts that made the difference, but the application of all of them. To this day I am not finished looking for better ways or systems. I am always thinking, "How can I be more efficient?" or "How can I improve on this system?" You should do the same in your family so that you are always adjusting your systems to meet the changing needs of your family.

Start to think of yourself as your family's life manager. Just like a manager of a business, you are managing the operation of your family's life, which is no small task. I have found that I now use my organizational and managerial skills more than I ever did in my former career as a professional manager.

How to make your home clutter-free

The first step in creating order in your home is to make the area where you and your family come into the house clutter free. This is the first impression you have on your home and can immediately set the mood for you, your spouse, and even your children. It is so easy to just kick off your shoes and drop your purse, kids' book bags, lunch boxes, etc., but this area needs to be set up so that it is done in an organized fashion. If you accomplish one thing today towards an organized home, this should be the one.

The space available in a home's entryway varies. Therefore, the ideas listed below may or may not work for your set up. You might need to adjust them to fit your house's layout, but the concept still remains the same.

Your entryway

➤ **Have a coat rack with a hook upon which each person in the family hangs his or her keys, book bags, lunch boxes, and coats.**

➤ **Have a basket for the children's shoes**. Make it a rule that your children must take off their shoes when they come inside to help keep the house clean. Utilizing a basket helps to keep the shoes together, and it offers a tidier look. Regular play shoes should be kept here, while dress shoes and shoes worn only once in a while should be kept in the closet.

➤ **Keep everything off the floor**. Try not to keep anything on the floor other than the shoe basket. Every book on feng shui talks about the negative energy created from having things all over the floor. If you can hang it up, do it. As your children's schoolwork increases and their book bags become too heavy for the hooks, they can keep their bags in their room to do homework and then bring them down at the end of the night so they are ready to go the next morning. If you have a closet in your entryway, you can place the heavier book bags there and then close the door to maintain a clean appearance. Space allowing, you may find that utilizing a cubby system to organize your things will help you to create order. Some even come with optional benches that are great for putting shoes on and off. Organizers such as this are increasing in popularity and can easily be found in home improvement stores or specialty catalogs.

After organizing your entrance hall, you can get started on taking control of the rest your house by taking a step back and really looking at your home. Where is the most clutter? What is the biggest weak spot in your house? The laundry room? The kitchen? For me, it was the laundry room. I easily do two loads of laundry a day and needed a better way to stay on top of it. I focused on this area first so I could quickly regain some order in this high-traffic area.

In this chapter, I will go room by room and discuss ways to organize and de-clutter each. Decide which room in your house needs the most attention first and start there. The order in which I cover each room may not be the order you will use, because your most disorganized room may be the one I mention last. I suggest fixing your room that needs the most attention first and working your way to the easiest room last. It is more motivating to continue through the rest of your home when you see dramatic results early on, and you will reap the rewards of your newly organized rooms sooner.

As you go through each room, sorting through and getting rid of items you no longer need or use is imperative to reclaiming order in your home. We all have things crammed in a drawer or closet that we do not need, even though we may refuse to admit it. Some of us have a harder time in this area than others, but you will find that the more you purge through your belongings, the easier it gets.

Take an honest look at your possessions and decide what they mean to you and your family. Does anyone still use that item? Does it work? Does it fit? Is it still in fashion? If the answer is "no" to any of these questions, then get rid of it.

I had a friend who once discovered she had six different curling irons stashed in her closet. She would upgrade her curling iron and then, since the old one was still operable, felt guilty about getting rid of it. Do not let yourself fall into that trap by letting things pile up on you. When you replace something you own with something better, donate, sell, or give away the original. Realize that it is still going to be put to good use and someone else will be very happy to receive it.

Donate it, give it to a friend or sell it

We do not help anyone if we have things in our closets or drawers that are not being used. Donating such items to charities is a great way to go. This way, someone else who is in need can benefit from your discarded items and you are not using precious storage space for something that is no longer needed in your family. You may even have friends that could use a certain item or piece of clothing that you no longer need. Be cautious of turning your old item into someone else's unwanted clutter, but if you know they want it, pass it on.

Churches, daycares, preschools, and the like are a great place to donate toys or even clothing that your children have outgrown. Many people will be excited to receive items that have served their time in your family but are of use to them. Check to see what types of things are needed, however, before you just drop off all of your unwanted items.

If you need the extra cash, consignments stores are a good

place to turn to. If you have nice clothes and toys that are still in good condition, you could make some pretty good money. Some places give you immediate cash, while others just give you store credit. Call ahead and find out the store's policy. You will also want to know if they prefer that the clothes be on hangers or just in a bag. Some stores have only certain days or times during which they accept potential consignment clothes, so be sure to ask before you go to avoid wasting a trip.

A garage sale is also an option if you have a lot of items to get rid of. Doing this with a friend or two will increase the amount of things to sell and can make your garage sale more successful. Advertise the items you know will sell fast to help generate traffic. Typically they are the higher end items such as large outdoor play toys, baby and children furniture, train tables, etc. Make sure you know what your neighborhood's policy is concerning garage sales and signage so you do not lose all your profit on fines. This happened to someone I knew and she was not happy about it because it actually created a loss instead of a profit for her.

Do take into consideration what your cost will be, including advertising, costs of the signs you put out (these are very helpful in helping people not only know that you are having a garage sale, but also in finding your house), and the time and energy you will spend putting it together. I have had several garage sales that went well, but as my family grew I realized that the return was no longer worth the effort. I then started donating, consigning, and passing on to friends the items I did not need anymore.

Another option for higher end items is to post them on eBay® to try to get top dollar for them. You can post them online yourself or utilize the stores that will take care of everything for you. Which method you use will depend on how many items you have to get rid of, your time constraints, and your financial situation.

When in doubt, throw it out

There are going to be some items that cannot be used again for one reason or another and just need to be put to rest. Get some large heavy-duty trash bags and pitch away. I always use a regular bag for items to donate and then a large black trash bag for the items that need to be thrown away. You may also put aside some things that need to be fixed. If you do not fix those items within a week, you may as well throw them out because they will probably never get fixed. Give yourself a deadline to do it, and if you do not meet your deadline then the item is not that important to you or it is no longer needed in your life.

➤ **Purging your belongings is an ongoing process.** First, you will need to do a major purging of your possessions. Then, once you have cleansed your home of the unnecessary items, you will have to check your home regularly to make sure you are not filling a closet or drawer that you just cleaned out with more stuff that you do not need. If you get a new toaster, do not put the old one in the cabinet or closet. Donate it if it still works or throw it out if it does not. You could also cut off the electrical cord for safety purposes and then give it to your curious children to take apart. Kids love to see how things work, and it is a form of recycling in an educational sort of way. (Please use common sense regarding what you give your children to play with and take all safety precautions.)

➤ **If you buy something new, get rid of something old.** You need to make space for your new purchase. Your house is not going to grow to accommodate what you have just brought into your home. If you buy a new clothing item, get rid of one you no longer wear. If you have tried on the same shirt again and again only to end up putting it back into the closet, it is a sign that you no longer need or want it. Do not just put it right back in your closet time and again. If you have not worn that item in a while, there must be a reason. The rule of thumb is if you have not worn it in two years, get rid of it.

It is hard to part with items we have spent money on or that have been given to us by a close friend, but it is an important part of keeping your house and mind clutter-free. Get rid of the old to make way for the new. You do not want to be wasteful by any means, but you do have to accept that some things need to go. Once you get going on this, it does get easier. You start to feel a sense of relief as you purge your space of old, broken, and outdated things. If it helps you, try to do it with a friend or family member who can help you keep things in perspective. It makes it a lot more fun as well as allowing you to accomplish more, faster. You could even trade time by having her help you through the purging process and then you could do the same for her.

Now that you have the mental mindset to take on the important task of reorganizing your home, let's take a look, room by room, to discuss how to regain order.

Simple ways to reorganize your home

Kitchen

In most, if not in all families, the kitchen is the room where you spend the most time and energy. Having your kitchen uncluttered and set up correctly significantly affects how your family operates. Everyone knows that people, even in a fancy social setting, tend to congregate in the kitchen. This is yet another reason why it is so important to analyze how your kitchen operates and the feel it gives to you, your family, and others.

➤ **What do you need on your countertop?** Take a step back and really study your kitchen's layout. What do you keep on your counter? Are they items that you frequently use? If you have something out that you rarely need, find a different place for it. I keep my toaster out because we use it almost daily. My parents, on the other hand, do not use their toaster very often, so they keep it out of sight in one of their cabinets. I do, however, keep my large KitchenAid® mixer out, even though I do not use it very often. I do this because it is too heavy to pull out whenever I need it and because I consider it a decorative item. Decide what you need easy access to and keep it on the counter. Put away those things that do not need to be taking up valuable space and creating clutter in your kitchen.

Once you have removed the unnecessary items from your kitchen counter, try to find space to display things that mean something to you and conjure good feelings when you see them. For example, on my windowsill I have photos of each of our children as well as one family shot. Whenever I am at the sink rinsing the never-ending pile of dishes, I look at those pictures and it makes me smile. Even when the kids are not behaving as they should, I get a burst of great love for them by looking at their adorable faces. Even though family photos are not functional in the true sense of the word, they need to be displayed in a prominent place to be enjoyed. Take care not to display so many that they create a cluttered space. Find your favorites and use those.

If you have the space to display cookbooks, pick out the ones you use the most and set them out so you can access them easily. Most cookbooks are so well illustrated on the cover that they also double as decoration and give your kitchen a warm feeling. It is great to use things that couple function with aesthetics.

No matter how small or large your kitchen is, keep it simple. You need lots of counter space to cook all those meals, so make sure you do not cover up what space you have, causing you to constantly work around things. Understand where you tend to do the most work in your kitchen and leave that area open. Display your cookbooks, etc. in areas that you do not use as much. A far-reaching corner is perfect for such items since it rarely gets used and fills in the empty space nicely.

➤ **Create work stations.** Next, think about your kitchen in terms of work stations. Place items that you use together close in proximity. If you use a breadbox, keep it by the toaster, since the two obviously go together. In my kitchen I have the toaster and the breadbox on the counter above my silverware drawer since I'm always reaching for a knife whenever I am using bread. It saves me just a few steps every time I make toast or a sandwich, but it all adds up.

Do you have your glasses and cups within reach of the refrigerator? After getting a glass, you almost always need to get ice or a drink from the refrigerator, so it makes sense to keep them close together. This saves some extra steps and also prevents your kitchen from being clogged up with people crossing paths. When I am in the kitchen cooking and my children come in for a drink, they can get what they need without me being in their way or vice versa. By setting up areas this way, children are in and out easily.

My children are still at the ages when they use plastic cups, so there are no broken glasses. Thus, I have created a drawer they can reach easily in which I store all of the plastic cups. I also put the plastic plates and bowls in the same drawer so that they can reach those as well. The more kid-friendly your kitchen is, the more self-sufficient your kids can be. This is not only better for you, but also for your children.

Listed are some quick tips to help organize your kitchen:

➤ **Use a large, deep drawer to store your plastic storage containers.** If you do not have one, purchase one or two large plastic tubs that you can slide onto the cabinet shelf. Make sure that it can easily be pulled out to get what you need. This helps prevent lost pieces and makes it easier to organize and access what you need.

➤ **Get a dispenser for your plastic grocery bags that can be hung on the inside of the pantry door or a cabinet.** There are many options out there, from fancy stainless-steel styles to the simple, inexpensive cloth dispensers. These bag dispensers cut back on the unruly bags that seem to breed themselves. This way you have all the bags you need, but they are neatly stored in the bag holders, which take up less space and are easier on the eyes. Do not keep the bags that held meat or milk because sometimes they can leak in the bags and will start to smell. Yes, that one is from personal experience!

➤ **Keep potholders and trivets in a drawer next to the stove for easy access.**

➤ **Keep items that are rarely used in the back of your cabinets or on the top shelf of high cabinets.** Save your prime real estate cabinet space for things you always use.

➤ **Have an established location for each item in your kitchen.** This helps you and your family quickly find items without having to search for something that is put in the wrong place. Make sure everyone knows where everything belongs. It makes it less frustrating for your "helpers" when they know exactly where everything is kept and makes them more likely to help out.

➤ **Use an index box with dividers for your recipes.**

➤ **Purchase or create your own notebook that has pockets and dividers to store and organize the recipes you tear out of magazines.** Do not just shove them in a cabinet or drawer. Sort them by food type so you can quickly retrieve one when you need it.

➤ **Purge items that you do not use.** Is it worth the space to store an item you rarely use, or are you better off without it? Be honest with yourself about what you must have in your kitchen and get rid of what you can do without.

➤ **Keep your coffee, filters, and coffee mugs in the cabinet above where you keep the coffee maker.** You should not have to walk all over the kitchen just to prepare a cup of coffee. Remember, every step counts!

➤ **Designate a certain shelf in your refrigerator for leftovers and store them all in glass or clear plastic containers so you know what is in there.** Keep your leftovers up on the top shelf so you can see through the bottom of the glass dish or plastic container. This way you know without removing the item and peaking in exactly what is in each container.

➤ **Have a designated place in your refrigerator for items used regularly.** For example, salad dressings should always be in the bottom door shelf lined up next to each other. This allows you to quickly get what you need without searching through the entire refrigerator. It also helps when making your grocery list because you can easily identify what you do and do not have. Regularly used items such as jelly, butter, mayonnaise, ketchup and mustard, etc. should always be kept in the same place. This is helpful in preventing the common phrase of, "Mom, where's the jelly?" Your children and spouse will always know where everything is. No more excuses about not being able to find what they need.

➤ **When you purchase more milk or eggs and the like, place the new container behind or under the older one.** Throwing out food because it expired is a waste of money and the time and energy it took to buy it and get it in your house. Do not restock an item in front of what you already have to prevent this.

➤ **Wipe down the shelves and walls of the refrigerator**

when your refrigerator is empty and you are due to go grocery shopping. If you do this before every big shopping trip, your refrigerator will maintain a clean look and stay sanitary.

➤ **Keep like items together in the refrigerator.** For example, all condiments that are commonly used together should be kept together. This way, in one quick grab you have everything you need.

➤ **Keep like items together in the freezer.** For the freezer, store all bulk meat together and frozen desserts together, etc. to save on search time. This helps to prevent finding filet mignons hidden in the back of your freezer from 12 months ago just to have to throw them out. You will not only be able to find what you need more easily, but also be aware of what you have.

➤ **Label bulk food that you store in the freezer with a permanent marker and include the date you froze it.** You may think that you will recall what you put in the freezer at the time, but two months down the road it will be difficult to remember what is what.

➤ **If you open an item that will rarely get used, use a marker and put the date you opened it on the label.** This way you will know when to pitch it. Just because the label has an expiration date, it does not always apply after it has been opened. This is great for spices since they lose their freshness after a year.

➤ **In your pantry, keep like items together, and if you have the space, organize them in straw or wicker style baskets.** This helps make it easier to keep the items sorted and is more aesthetically pleasing. For the safety of your children, store glass jars and bottles up high so they do not accidentally break, and keep food items packaged in boxes and bags down low.

➤ **Store the items that you allow your children to prepare and eat at their eye level.** You can even have a "snack basket" of items that they are allowed to eat. Empty the individually packaged items such as granola bars or pretzels into the basket so your kids can quickly grab a healthy snack on their own.

➤ **Pour foods that easily go stale or are hard to store into sealed plastic tubs.** Put cereal, crackers, sugars, flour, etc. in these types of containers. It helps them last longer and fit neatly in your pantry. You can even get the kind that stack to maximize your space even more.

➤ **Use tiered shelving in your pantry to position items so that you can see their labels and create more space.** These are great for cans and spices.

➤ **Store items that you rarely use in the back of your pantry.** Make sure, however, that you can still see them so you do not forget they are there.

➤ **Keep items that are considered treats and are rarely consumed on higher shelves.** Items such as cookies should be kept out of reach of little hands. This also keeps them out of sight so that your children (and you) are not tempted to eat them more than they should.

➤ **Turn your junk drawer into a "utility drawer."** Just by using the name "junk drawer" you are setting yourself up to have a drawer that can barely be opened with miscellaneous stuff in it. Give it the name it deserves. Start by having dividers in the drawer to store the basics such as scissors, tape, a few pens, and a pad of paper, but do not let it become a catchall. You would not cram all types of papers or other random items in your silverware drawer, so resist the temptation to put them in your "utility drawer." Most of the items you try to quickly shove in this drawer already have a home elsewhere; just put them where they belong in the first place.

Laundry Room

This is a very high-traffic area in any house, no matter how large a family is, and it needs to be set up to run efficiently.

I have lived in many homes with laundry rooms that have ranged from the size of a walk-in pantry to the size of a large bedroom. Through this I have learned that no matter what size laundry room you have, the basic steps of keeping it organized are still the same.

When we lived in our house with a very small laundry room, I had to get rid of our laundry basket due to lack of space. At first this was a challenge, but when we moved to our next house that had an unusually large laundry room, I did not bring a laundry basket back into use even though I had ample space. I did, of course, have hampers for the dirty clothes, but nothing for the clean clothes. I discovered that by not using a laundry basket to load up with clean clothes that needed folding, I folded the clothes right out of the dryer and never had baskets of laundry that needed tending to. This technique also decreased the amount of ironing I needed to do because the clothes did not wrinkle as badly as they did sitting in a stuffed basket.

If you like to fold clothes somewhere else in the house, you may need a basket to transport them, but be careful and do not fall into the trap of thinking "I'll fold those later when I have more time," because you won't have more time. One of the biggest steps to staying organized is doing what needs to be done right then. If it is time to transfer wet clothes into the dryer, then it is time to fold the dry clothes to make room. If you ever do want to fold somewhere else, just make two trips and carry them by the armful. It is best not to fold clothes in other rooms if you can help it because all it does is mess up other places in the house. If you are not able to put the clothes away immediately you will have a mess all over the family room or wherever else you may be working. And we all know the odds of them getting knocked over by your children are very high.

What you will need:

➤ **A place to hang clothes.** Even if you only have space for a small bar to hang clothes on, it is worth having. This allows you to hang clothes right when they come out of the dryer to help reduce wrinkling as well as being more efficient because you do not waste time folding a shirt that is going to be hung in a closet. Never double handle anything if you can help it. You will hear this stated more than once. The hanging bar can also be a place to hang wet items that need to dry if you do not have room for a drying rack.

➤ **A medium-sized basket for each family member.** Having a basket for each family member is a very helpful way to not only sort out clothes, but also to carry them to the appropriate rooms. You can use just one for you and your spouse or you may prefer to use two, depending on your space and the amount of laundry you both produce.

The baskets should allow your children to easily carry up their laundry to be put away and then returned empty to get filled again. You can also put miscellaneous toys and items that are found around the house in the basket of its respective owner. This helps prevent piles at the bottom of the stairs (or anywhere else) of random toys and also helps keep the house picked up without having to run from room to room all day.

I use jute baskets that are about 12" × 12". Wicker, canvas or straw baskets will work well too; just make sure the clothes that are in them cannot get picked. You may choose a larger basket than I have, but for space considerations and because they should be emptied frequently, you do not want them to be too big. When your baskets are the size of the ones I use, you tend to empty them more often than when you have a lot of extra space to fill.

Your children should get into the habit of putting away their own clothes at an early age. My three-year-old can carry up his basket, and with my help, put everything away. He sorts the shirts and shorts, etc. and then I help him put them neatly in his drawers. Remember, your children are never too young to learn how to help out around the house. They will need help at first, but it will pay off tremendously in the long run. You will need to follow up with them for a while. After my five-year-old never seemed to have clean clothes, I finally realized that he had been emptying his basket behind a chair pushed against the wall. When I discovered how he was putting away his clothes so quickly, it explained everything. It took a couple of weeks of inspecting his drawers after he put his clothes away, but he finally got it right once he realized that I was going to follow through to make sure he put everything away properly.

➤ **Designated space for your laundry soaps.** Ideally you should put your soaps in cabinets in your laundry room. If you do not have a cabinet for the laundry soaps, purchase a large wicker or a straw-style basket to keep them together and organized. You can place it on a counter or on top of your washer if it is a front-end loader. If you have to store your soap in view, keep the powder detergents in plastic storage containers. This helps prevent boxes of detergent from tearing and spilling and gives your laundry room a cleaner and more organized appeal.

➤ **Two dirty clothes hampers.** Get one dark colored hamper in which to place dark clothes and one white hamper for your white clothes. This system allows even the youngest of children to sort dirty clothes by color. It also allows you to save time by not having to sort and re-sort your colors when trying to do a load of laundry.

Get creative with decorating your laundry room and give it the same attention that you would any other room in your house. You are in the laundry room more than many other rooms, yet typically, there is no care as to how it is decorated. Be creative and create a space you like to be in!

If you have the luxury to repaint your laundry room, choose a fun and cheery color. A soft yet energetic yellow always brightens a room and lifts spirits. Who wants to do laundry in a room that is painted a dull or depressing color? Once I approached my laundry room as a legitimate room and decorated it as such, my whole laundry experience changed. In our super-sized laundry room I had a magazine rack hanging on the wall, a craft and homework table, a built-in desk, cozy carpet that the kids loved to lounge on, and tons pictures of our family on the wall. I would have never guessed that our laundry room would have been the room that everyone liked to hang out in most, but it was. This taught me something and opened my eyes about this functional room and its importance.

Your laundry room does not have to be super-sized to be a fun room. Regardless of what amount of space you have, just make it one that you enjoy being in. Paint it a fun color, hang some family photos on the wall, and create a space that you enjoy.

Bathrooms

➤ **In each bathroom, store pre-moistened cleaning wipes for quick cleanups.** Use these easy cleanup products to do a once over while the children are in the bathtub—age appropriate of course. You are right there to insure they are safe but are also cleaning at the same time. With older children they can also use these to easily help in keeping their bathroom clean.

➤ **Make sure to utilize the cabinet space under all the bathroom sinks for storage.** Toilet paper is not the only thing you can keep under the sink. I store extra paper towel rolls in my guest bath because I always tend to have extra room in that cabinet and it is not too far from the kitchen. This can also be a great place to store cleaning supplies. Use tiered shelving to help maximize the storage space.

➤ **If you have a lot of drawers in your bathrooms use them**

efficiently. Drawers are a wonderful way to organize all of the toiletries you need, so consider yourself lucky if you have an ample supply of them. Organize each drawer by like item. For example, in your master bathroom, use one drawer for makeup, another for nail polish and any other related nail products, another for hair brushes and accessories, and one for facial products such as cleansers and moisturizers, etc. Decide what you use regularly, divide everything by category, and then separate them into drawers. If you do not have drawers or only have a few, use a riser to create more space under the sink and utilize small plastic baskets to sort your products.

➤ **Be creative and utilize the cabinet space in your children's bathrooms.** Many times space is wasted when your children are younger or if you have only boys in a bathroom; they tend to use fewer products than girls do. For example, I use two of the drawers in my child's bathroom to store his underwear and pajamas. I am short on space in his bedroom because he shares the room with his brother and we do not have enough chests-of-drawers for all of their clothes. This works out well because when he gets out of the tub, his clothes for bed are right there at his fingertips. Think outside the box when it comes to maximizing your storage space.

➤ **Keep a clothes hamper in each bathroom to make it easy to put dirty clothes in the appropriate place.** Make the basket manageable for your children to carry so they can easily take it to the laundry room to unload.

➤ **Use hooks or pegs to make hanging up wet towels or bathrobes easy.** Understand that kids will keep things more organized and tidier if you make it easy for them. My kids will not fold the towels back on the towel bar as I prefer them to but they can easily hang them on a hook. As long as it is off the floor, it looks pretty good and I will not complain because I know they tried.

➤ **Keep a toilet brush in each bathroom for easy cleaning.** They are not expensive and are worth the extra cost so you do not have to carry the brush from one bathroom to the next.

➤ **Use liquid soap dispensers by the sink.** They do not leave the soap residue like traditional bars and do not harbor the germs that can grow on soap bars. Use the large refillable soaps versus buying a new dispenser every time you run out so it is more economical and environmentally friendly.

Closets

Closets, by nature, have interesting connotations about them. You hear of people having "skeletons in their closets" or someone being a "closet smoker." A closet is where you keep things that you may not otherwise want people to know about or see.

You are about to change that in regards to the closets in your home. When a person has an organized closet, it is indicative that the rest of that person's home is organized as well. No more slowly opening your closet doors with the fear that you will be crushed to death by an avalanche of items. In your newly organized home, your closets will be neatly laid out with everything you need right at your fingertips. Just follow these simple steps and you will have a closet that you will be so proud of, you will not even need a door to cover it.

➤ **Install closet organizers.** If your closets do not already have space organizers or at least a double hanging bar in it, it is worth your time and money to install them. Having the traditional single bar with a shelf on top wastes a lot of space that you could utilize if you had the organizers. Be thoughtful about who is using the closet and how it is used so that you install the system that works best.

➤ **In your children's closet, hang the dressier, seldom worn, and off-season clothes on the higher bar.** Make sure your children can reach the clothes on the bottom that they wear every day. Keep their nicer play clothes hanging on the bottom bar in the closet and fold the regular play clothes that can get dirty in the chest-of-drawers. It is always good to protect several outfits for your children to wear for nicer outings. Typically, kids do not go for the clothes that are hanging up as much as they do the ones that are in the drawers.

➤ **Try rolling your children's t-shirts and placing them in the drawers so they can see more than just what is on top.** This helps your children wear more of their clothes because they can see everything they have.

➤ **Hang organizers on the walls or door of the closet.** Belt racks and hat racks work wonders. Clear pocket holders that can hang on the back of the door are great for mittens, gloves, hats, scarves, socks, etc. Utilize the wall space as much as possible.

➤ **Use shoe or sweater holders to organize outfits for each day of the week.** If your children do not wear uniforms, have them help pick out the outfits they want to wear that week. They can switch the outfits around for a particular day, but insist they stick to whatever was originally chosen for the week to prevent time-consuming clothing battles on school mornings.

➤ **Store shoes that are only used for special occasions in their boxes marked with their description.** Store the shoe boxes on a high shelf so that they are out of the way yet can be quickly identified by reading the description on the box.

➤ **Stuff tissue paper in purses that are not in season to help maintain their shape.** Place them up high or safely on the back of a shelf until next season.

➤ **Try to keep as much as you can off the closet floor.** Shoes are the only items that should be on the floor, but even then they should be placed neatly on shoe racks. If you must store them directly on the floor, make sure they are neatly lined up with the front of the shoes facing outward so you can easily see what style they are. Do not just throw the shoes on the floor because it looks chaotic, makes it harder to find what you are looking for, and it is not good for the life of your shoes.

➤ **If you have a walk-in closet, hang up a picture or two and make it fun.** If you have the extra wall space for pictures or photos that do not have a home elsewhere, hang them in your walk-in closets to add a little personality.

➤ **Use wood hangers in the master closet.** Wood hangers prevent your closet from becoming crammed and wrinkling all of your clothes. They also let the garments hang better and protect the life of your clothes. Wood hangers are more expensive but can be found at discount and home improvement stores at a fair price. If you need to spread out the cost, buy 20 or so at a time and slowly switch your closet over to all wood hangers. You can give your plastic hangers to your oldest children who may be outgrowing the smaller plastic ones. There is a reason that all closet organizer ads use the wood hangers; they not only look more organized and are more pleasing to the eye, but they are also better for your clothes.

➤ **Organize the clothes in your closet by color and style.** Being particular in sorting your clothes saves you a lot of time when picking out outfits. Organize your closet by style and then color. First, put all of your sleeveless shirts together and then group them by color from lightest to darkest. Then do the same with your short-sleeved shirts and then your long-sleeved shirts, sorting them all from lightest to darkest. Dresses, skirts, and pants can also be sorted by style and then color. This may sound tedious, but once you have set up your closet this way you will realize how helpful it is. You will not have to push your way through your clothes looking for a particular item. You will be able to just stand back and see everything and easily grab what you need. You will wear more of your clothes because you can easily choose from what you have and will be able to create a variety of outfits more easily. In the end, this decreases the need to shop more because you are able to make better use of what you have.

➤ **Store out-of-season clothing in a separate closet.** The climate where you live will determine how much of your wardrobe you need to store elsewhere. For example, because I live in a milder climate, in the winter I only put away my linen clothes or clothes that are obviously for the summer only. I leave out my tank tops and short sleeve shirts to use for layering. Move the items you know you will not wear that season to another closet, but do not put away things that can be incorporated into other outfits. If you do not have an extra closet, try to place those items in the back of your closet so they are out of the way.

➤ **Place your purses on a shelf where you can easily see them.** This helps to match your purse with the outfit you are going to wear. You will end up carrying the same bag every time if you cannot easily grab another one. If you prefer to use one bag all of the time, choose one that has black and brown in it to go with everything in the winter and a light neutral bag for the warmer months. This is good if you are on a tight budget or have limited closet space to store your purses. It also saves you the time of switching everything from one bag to the next.

➤ **If you repeatedly put on an outfit just to decide you do not like it, it is time to get rid of it.** Do not put back in your closet the same shirt time after time, only to never wear it and have it take up your precious closet space. If you do not love how it looks on you, why keep it? Keep the clothes that look great on you and not the ones that are just OK. Take it to a consignment store or donate it. Someone else will be thrilled with it, and you and your closet will be better for it.

➤ **Use matching baskets or other organizers for hard-to-store items.** These containers can be stored on a top shelf yet can be easily accessed when needed. They are perfect for items such as bathing suits, pantyhose, and the like that are difficult to store and not used every day. I prefer the ones that you cannot see into but have labels so you know what is in them. This eliminates the cluttered look of the clear containers through which one can see all the mess that is inside of them.

➤ **When you take an item off its hanger, put the hanger in a designated spot on the beginning or end of the clothes bar.** Do not put the empty hanger back where you got it from. Keeping your empty hangers together prevents your closet from being randomly stuffed with empty hangers and eliminates the search to find those hangers when you need them. Do this and then every so often grab the empty hangers and take them to the laundry room to be used on the clothes that come out of the dryer.

➤ **Have a designated spot for clothes that need to be hand washed or dry-cleaned.** This way you can easily grab your clothes for the cleaners when you are headed out the door, and it prevents items that need special care from accidentally ending up in your washer.

➤ **Keep your hall closet from being a catch-all.** Store coats in this closet and use the shelf space wisely. Organizing what you keep in this closet is important to keeping it orderly and being able to find what you need when you need it. Utilize plastic tubs and label what is stored in each so you can quickly find what you need.

Bedrooms

Each bedroom will need to be organized differently depending on whose room it is. First, I will discuss the children's bedrooms, because these are the rooms that can get the craziest.

The cleanliness of a child's room is an ongoing battle for parents, and there is a limit to what you can do or expect. You can help, however, by having their rooms set up so that keeping them neat and organized is a much easier task.

➤ **Control the clutter by utilizing organizers.** You must take into consideration the age of your children and how they live in their rooms. If it is a young child who still has a lot of toys, labeled plastic tubs displayed on shelves are perfect to help create order to his belongings. These types of containers can be found in catalogs and in home improvement stores. You can spend a fortune on them in higher-end catalogs and stores or just buy the basic plastic tubs on stacked shelves. No matter what storage container you choose, it will be worth the money. It enables even the youngest of children to put away their toys in an organized manner. You can label what goes in each container or even put a photo of what belongs for the child who cannot read yet.

➤ **Limit the amount of toys and other items your children accumulate.** The amount of toys that are in a child's room has a direct effect on its organization. My husband used to always point this out to me when I would complain about the mess in our boys' rooms. He was right. If a child has 10 toys that each contain 150 pieces, that's 1,500 little pieces that can easily get scattered across the room. Yes, I know that children should always put away one toy before they get out another, and maybe yours do, but the reality for us was that it did not always happen. In fact, it rarely happened unless I was right there policing their playtime. Choose with your child some favorite toys that he really wants to keep in his room and clear out the rest.

➤ **Designate a closet with a high shelf for some of the puzzles, games, or other toys that contain a lot of pieces.** This allows you to pull out one toy at a time in a more controlled environment and ensures that everything gets put away properly. This not only keeps your house tidier but also prevents pieces from getting lost.

➤ **Use a toy box.** A toy box can be a great way to make cleanup time easier, especially if it has a lid to conceal the toys. Toy boxes work best for larger items such as dolls or stuffed animals, but not for small pieces that will only get lost on the bottom. Make sure it does not become a catch-all by going through it with your child periodically to pull out what may not belong.

➤ **Adjust your children's furniture to accommodate their needs as they age.** As your children get older, the functions of their bedrooms change. There are fewer toys, but there is still a mess. Laundry and other unrecognizable items are all over the floor. The mess is still there, it is just in a different form. Having furniture that accommodates what is important to a middle-school-aged child or teenager helps to keep the room organized. A desk with drawers to organize schoolwork does wonders, and a magazine rack for all of those magazines helps keep clutter off the floor. Have your child work with you to determine what type of storage containers or furniture might help keep order in his room. Let your child, whatever his age, play an active role in reorganizing his room. He can give you insight into what will work best for how he lives and plays in his room. This will increase the odds of keeping things orderly. If you reorganize the room one day when he is at school, your chances that your child will keep things the way you want are not as great as if you have him participate in the process.

➤ **Make your master bedroom your sanctuary.** This is the one place that should be an escape from the many toys and clutter that can be created from raising a family. Hopefully, the master bedroom is not a big weakness depending on your innate organizational skills. This room should be as clutter-free as possible to help you unwind at the end of the day and to keep your mind clear. It is the first thing you wake up to and the last place you see when you go to bed at the end of the day. You do not want the environment there to be one of chaos and clutter. Keep it simple, and keep it clean.

➤ **Make the master bedroom a "no toy" zone.** Once your children hit the appropriate age, about two or three years old, do not allow any toys to be in your bedroom. There are plenty of places in the house to play, and your room should not be one of them. Once we enforced this rule, our room became an adult haven. When your children are very young, this is next to impossible, in fact, we use to have a basket of toys in the room when the kids were toddlers so that they would stay safe and entertained while we got dressed. You know the ages of your children and the stage of life you are in. Decide what works best for your family now. When they are little, having things in the master bedroom can help your life, but as they get older, there is no longer a need for it. At that point, instill the "no toy" rule. When one of our children walk into our room with a toy in hand, they know they are about to get redirected. They can put the toy away and then come back in to talk to us, but not until then.

➤ **The master bedroom's focus should be about you and your spouse.** The photographs in the master bedroom should be only of you and your spouse. This means no photos of your children. I am sure that some of you are thinking that I am way off base because your children are a part of you and your spouse and are the most important thing in your life. That is all very true, but your relationship with your spouse is also extremely important and you should have one room that is only about the two of you. This is where you display pictures of you and your spouse as a couple. I know it is hard to find pictures of the two of you without any children in them, but search hard. I even deliberately have people take pictures of my husband and me knowing that I will use it in our bedroom to update the old one.

➤ **Have a designated place for your books and magazines.** If you love to read in your room, do not stack up all of the books and magazines on your nightstand. If you do not have an available drawer in your nightstand to keep them in, use a magazine rack to help keep your reading material orderly. Realize too, that you can only read so much. If your third issue of the same magazine has arrived and you have not read the others, understand that some need to get pitched because you will never catch up. Try to develop the skill of scanning a magazine for articles that are of interest to you, rip them out and then toss the rest of the magazine. Put the article somewhere you know you will read it. This helps you to find quickly what is important to you in a magazine and it takes up a lot less space than holding on to the entire publication.

Family room

By definition, this is a room for the whole family to enjoy and should be set up accordingly. This does not mean that it should be full of toys and clutter but be organized so that the family can spend quality time together in it.

➤ **Create a room that is family friendly yet still clutter-free.** Designate a closet shelf, drawer, or basket to store items such as games, puzzles, and books that can be enjoyed as a family. This is a great room for such family activities, but it does not have to be taken over by toys. Keep the games, puzzles, etc. available but neatly out of sight. This allows the room to maintain an orderly appearance but still be very functional for your family.

➤ **Beware of coffee table clutter.** It is nice to have decorative pieces, photographs, and magazines displayed on your coffee or end tables, but do not let it get out of control. You should have about three magazines on a table and not 20. Use a magazine rack if you receive a lot of magazines and catalogs to keep them off of your furniture. You do not want to take up every inch of space on your tables to help keep a clean look and keep it functional. You want it to be easy to use a coffee table for an impromptu card or board game.

➤ **Keep the toys to a minimum.** Have limitations in this room, even though it is the family room. We allow the kids to bring out one toy at a time in this room such as Lego's or Lincoln Logs, but they know it all has to be put away when they are finished playing with it. This is great room to do things as a family, but it is in a more controlled environment as compared to the children's bedrooms, and the expectations should be different.

Living and dining rooms

What do you say here? Kids do not really need to be in these rooms unless it is appropriate to the event. I love having meals in our dining room once a week to help my children learn the correct table manners in a formal setting, but it is not a room in which they should play or hang out. The living room is the same way. The children can go in there to read with my husband or me, but it is not a room for them to play in at will.

The organization of these rooms should be very simple. Usually, there is not much clutter or mess by the nature of the room. Sometimes when our house is not up to my standard, I like to escape to our living room after the children have gone to bed and read or enjoy a glass of wine. It allows me to recharge without being surrounded by the reminders of what I should be doing in our house. The living room is also a great place to visit with your spouse after a day's work because it should be clean and orderly, and thus peaceful and relaxing.

Tips to help stay organized

Now that you have reorganized each room in your house, you should be feeling some sense of order. This is the first step to effectively managing your home as well your family's life, and it is a very important one. As I mentioned earlier in the book, a one-time reorganization of your house is not the cure-all. Every day you have to live an organized life. Some days will be more successful than others, but if you are able keep your house together for the most part, you will not lose control over it ever again. When unexpected guests drop by, you will not hide and pretend not to be there for the fear that they will see your house turned upside down. Your house will always have a sense of order to it, and it will take but just minutes to clean it up quickly.

There are a few basic principles to maintaining organization and keep your house clutter-free. Follow these simple steps to maintain the order in your home you have finally created.

➤ **Have a place for everything, and put everything in its place.** We have all heard it before, and it is very true. If you do not have a spot for a particular item, you will deal with that item over and over again. You will see it on the counter, wonder where to put it, delay the decision, and then just leave it there. Your subconscious will think about it every time you look at it, and it will bother you until it is dealt with. You may not even be aware that you are thinking about that item or that it is affecting your mood, but it is. Make the decision to find a place for it and put it away. Delaying that decision is a form of procrastination and ultimately leads to clutter.

➤ **Put all of your owner's manuals in a labeled plastic tub with a lid.** This is a great tip to implement. If you have one designated place for all of the owner's manuals you get, you will never have to search for one when you need it. This also prevents the manuals from being crammed in random drawers and closets, creating clutter and to never be found again.

➤ **Do not double handle anything.** Once you have established where everything belongs, there is no need to double handle anything. Before you set something down on the counter, a chair, or any other place it does not belong, think about where it is supposed to be. Put it there right then; do not set it down temporarily to be put away later. If you cannot decide where it is that item is supposed to be, maybe it does not belong in your house at all.

➤ **Sort through your mail right when you get it.** Have a designated spot for your mail, your spouse's mail, and your children's mail. Pitch the items that you know are junk mail right when you go through it. Do not set it aside to go through later. Ideally, you would read your mail right then and toss what is not important. If you cannot attend to it immediately, put it in a designated spot where you know it is safe until you can get to it. Flip through the catalogs that may be of significance to you. If you are not looking to purchase anything at the time, just throw them all away. Just because they are mailed to you does not mean you have to go through every single one. Do not pile them up to be looked at later. (I must confess, however, that I like to go through a few of the fashion-forward catalogs even if I am not looking to buy just to keep up with the season's new styles.)

➤ **Have a minimum standard on high-traffic areas such as the kitchen, laundry room, and family room, and stick to them.** Even on the weekends or in the summer, let your family know that no one can play until the basics are done so there is some order maintained in the house. If you always maintain your minimum standard, things cannot get out of control.

An example of this is requiring that the table and counters be cleaned off completely after lunch or snack before the children can go outside.

➤ **Try to do what you can today, right now, and avoid putting off things until tomorrow.** A lot of times it is easier to just do something right then versus thinking about it, trying to decide when you will do it, being frustrated that it is not done, and then going through the whole thought process again the next day. You will realize that some things are far easier to just do rather than to give it a lot of thought time.

It is like the bulb that needs to be changed. Each time you turn on that light switch, you think, "I really need to change that bulb," and then you don't. But you think about it every time and it can go on for days and days until it becomes an annoyance. If you spent the few minutes to just change the bulb when it went out, you would never think about it again. As a parent, you have better things to put your thoughts into than a burned out bulb that never gets changed. Apply this same concept to everything that you need to do. Obviously, this cannot apply to large projects such as painting a porch, but for the little tasks that come up daily, it is very effective.

2

Easy Solutions to Help You Keep Your Home Clean

NOW THAT YOU HAVE YOUR HOME ORGANIZED, IT WILL HELP to decrease the amount of time you spend cleaning. Now you have a basic standard of order in your home, and you will not have to pick up clutter and sort through a mess in order to clean. This will save you a lot of time and help you to clean more effectively.

Create a cleaning system

The best way to approach cleaning your home is to come up with a system that works for you and then stick to it. If you do not already have a cleaning system in place, try these suggestions for a while and then adjust them to suit your preferences. You may find that you have a better way that works for your family and lifestyle, but at least you will have gotten into a routine of systematic cleaning. The goal is to find a routine and system that allows you to maintain a clean home with the least effort and frustration.

➤ **Use the one-project approach.** Some people like cleaning one room at a time. I found, however, that this did not work for me. I like to pick a single task and apply it to the entire house all at once. If I am in the toilet-cleaning mode and have a toilet brush and cleaner in hand, I feel I might as well clean all of the toilets in the house. This is my least favorite household chore, so I like to get it out of the way all at once. In fact, I always schedule this chore after I have gone running or to the gym, because I am already sweaty and due for a shower. When I come home, I immediately clean the bathrooms and then hop into the shower. Do your dirty work when you are already dirty anyway.

You can also use the one-project approach with chores such as vacuuming. If you have the vacuum out, do not just vacuum one room, do the whole house. Approaching housework this way saves time because if you have the appliance or supplies out for a certain job and complete them all at once, you will not waste your energy pulling out and putting things away.

➤ **Schedule the days you deep clean.** Look at your schedule and decide which days are better for you to designate to cleaning. Whether you are a working or stay-at-home parent, it should be obvious to you the best times for a good deep cleaning. You may find that you like to do a little every day to get it all done, or you may prefer to knock it all out in one day.

I used the a-little-every-day approach for a while and it got old fast because I felt like I was always doing housework. We all know that you are cleaning and doing laundry just to maintain basic order in your home on a daily basis, and the addition of deep-cleaning every day became overwhelming for me. I felt like I was always working and in the house and losing time with my family. Once I changed my system to allow for deep cleaning on Mondays and Tuesdays only, I felt some relief. I knew that on those two days I would crank it out in the morning while my oldest three children were in school and I had my three-year-old as a helper. I worked hard and fast, and got it done. Then the rest of the week, even though I was still doing basic cleaning, the major cleaning was complete and I felt free to do other things.

My children even know that Monday is their deep-cleaning day. They do basic chores around the house all week, but this is their day to do the extra things that need to be accomplished. (Refer to "Recruiting help from your family," which is discussed later in this chapter). I like Mondays for cleaning because typically the house needs it after the weekend. I could never manage to do it all in one day, especially with my youngest child at home, so having the second day, Tuesday, to complete everything was necessary.

If you have a designated time set aside for cleaning, you know it will get done and do not have to spend time wondering how or when you will ever do it all. Protect those cleaning times so you do not get off of your schedule. If you do not have to make an appointment or go grocery shopping, etc. during that time, don't. Protect that time like you would a doctor's appointment so you always know it will get done and you will have the time to do it. Understand that I do not mean that you should miss something important at your child's school just to clean. Rather, I am saying that if something isn't very important, do whatever it is another time so you can stick to your schedule.

General cleaning tips

➤ **Decide which days you will commit to cleaning and schedule them on your family calendar and day planner.** This way you will know not to plan anything that can wait until another day on those designated cleaning days. You may clean on one or two days depending on your family's schedule.

➤ **Keep your cleaners together in a plastic tub with a handle so you can easily grab everything you need.** It is more efficient and keeps your cleaning cabinet neat, tidy, and free of those nasty rust stains some cleaners can leave behind. Put some rubber gloves and rags in your cleaning tub as well so you have everything you need. If you do not use rubber gloves to clean, you should. It protects your hands from harsh chemicals that can dry out your skin as well as expose you to potentially toxic chemicals.

➤ **Use as many all-purpose cleaners as you can so you do not have a lot of different cleaners to contend with.** Some of the job-specific cleaners are unnecessary and just take up space. Use products that have multiple uses and do not forget about household products such as vinegar and baking soda. They make for great cleaners and are both inexpensive and environmentally friendly.

➤ **Teach your children how to use a small hand vacuum at an early age**. Kids love to use them and they come in handy to pick up small messes.

➤ **The less clutter you have, the easier it will be to clean**. Display only items that matter to you and those you do not mind cleaning around. You want your house to have personality and a decorative flare, but you do not want items scattered everywhere that have no meaning to you yet add to your cleaning time.

➤ **Purchase cleaning tools that are easy for your children and you to use for quick clean ups**. Items such as the disposable cleaning cloths and the Swiffer®-style sweepers for floors are great because they allow children to pitch in without the potential mess of traditional cleaners. Feather dusters are another great and easy tool for children to use.

➤ **Make cleaning easy for you**. The easier you can make cleaning for you, the more you will do it. If you have a two-story house, keep one vacuum downstairs and another one upstairs. Yes, you will have the added cost of an additional vacuum, but you will be far more inclined to use it because you do not have to lug a heavy vacuum up the stairs and then back down again. It will also save your back.

➤ **When your family is going on an outing together, ask your spouse to load the kids in the car while you do a quick pick up in the kitchen and family room**. This is a great way to do a quick clean when your children are young and you are too short on time to do it before you leave. This way, when you return, the house looks great. I love doing this before we leave for church or go out of town. The quick five minutes I spend on the house really lets us re-enter with a better attitude and creates some order in the home.

➤ **Work fast!** Realize that the time you save by moving faster while you clean the house will be time that you can spend doing what you really want to do.

➤ **Set a time limit in each room to clean in the morning.** Once my family leaves for school, I know I will spend 15 minutes working in the kitchen and then 10 minutes in the laundry room. After that, I finish getting myself ready for the day or catch up on my personal to-do lists. What is not done after that set time limit will be completed later. This prevents you from focusing too much time in a given area just to neglect other things that must get tended to as well.

➤ **Enforce a "no-shoes-in-the-house" policy.** This dramatically reduces the amount of dirt on your floors and furniture as well as being much more sanitary. Keep a basket by the door where you enter and ask your children to remove their shoes as they come into the house. Bonus: You will always know where your children's shoes are and stop the endless searches for them as you head out the door. I love it when, if my children complain that they cannot find their shoes, I quickly remind them that if they had put their shoes where they belonged in the first place, they would not need to search for them at all.

➤ **Let your children use easy slip-on shoes or rain boots to play outside.** This helps enforce the "no-shoes-in-the-house" rule because they can be put on and off quickly and also helps children who cannot tie their own shoes. The easier you make it for your children to follow the rules, the more likely they will be to do it.

➤ **When you refill your vacuum with your last vacuum bag, put the empty package with your grocery list.** This way, when you go shopping the next time, you will be able to restock on the bags before you need them. I have learned that you cannot always find the type of bags that you need, and this way you have some extra time to ensure you can find the kind that fits your vacuum. You also do not get stuck at home with an over-stuffed vacuum bag without any extras to switch it out with. (To avoid this issue all together, buy a bag-less vacuum.)

Room-by-room cleaning guide

Kitchen

➤ **Use one kitchen dishrag for the entire day, and then after supper use it to spot clean your kitchen floor.** Then toss it in the dirty laundry. This buys you time until you are able to mop the entire floor.

➤ **Establish a routine for when you load and unload the dishwasher.** For example, I always have a load washing at the end of the night, and then in the morning I use the clean items to set the breakfast table and unload the rest while my children eat.

➤ **Try not to load the dishwasher with dishes that do not**

need a deep cleaning or take up too much space. If you measure rice or water in a measuring cup or measuring spoons, they really do not need to go through a full dishwasher cycle. Just rinse them and they are ready to be used again. If you have a large item to clean, you are better off hand washing it instead of putting in your dishwasher, where it will take up valuable space that can be used for lots of smaller items. Doing this prevents a sink of dirty dishes while you are running another load in the dishwasher.

➤ **Save on washing cups by assigning each child a certain colored one.** The child will always know which cup is his and can use it throughout the day for drinks. Rinse it out each time and set it next to the sink to be used again. (Do not do this if there is an illness going around in the family.)

➤ **Keep paper plates and small disposable cups for easy cleanup when you are in a big hurry or do not want a sink full of dirty dishes while a load is running in your dishwasher.**

➤ **Use a paper towel as a plate for quick sandwiches and snacks.** It saves on dishes and is a plate and napkin all rolled into one.

➤ **Sanitize your kitchen counter thoroughly on a regular basis.** It can harbor just as many if not more germs than a bathroom. Do not save this for a weekly deep clean. A hot, soapy rag can help eliminate many of those germs and can easily be done nightly after supper. You can even toss a dishrag in the microwave for a few seconds to get it extra hot to help kill germs.

Bathrooms

➤ **Use your washcloth to wipe down your bathroom sink and counter.** When you switch out your facial washcloth, which should be often, put some soap on it and use it to wipe down the sink and counters. Using a new washcloth for your face every couple of days is important to prevent bacterial growth from being transferred back onto your skin. I once had an esthetician tell me she used a new washcloth every time she washed her face for this reason. Just think how clean her bathroom sink would be if she used this rule!

➤ **Clean the bathroom while your child bathes.** If your child is old enough to bathe without constant assistance or supervision, yet you still need to be in the bathroom with him, this can be a great time for cleaning. Keep some cleaners safely tucked away in your child's bathroom so you can clean while he is bathing. While he is splashing away in the tub, you can have the entire bathroom (minus the tub, of course) blitzed. It is win-win situation because you are with him to ensure his safety, able to chat, and you are able to get some much-needed cleaning accomplished. Remember, this is only for children who are old enough to be in the tub or shower without your constant eye on them.

➤ **If you have a clear shower door, use a squeegee to wipe it down after you shower.** This dramatically cuts down on soap scum, which saves time when you deep clean. Even younger children think it is fun to do after they shower. The novelty will be gone by the time they are teenagers, but at least they are in the habit of doing it.

➤ **Wipe down the tub after each use with the washcloth you used to bathe.** This is not as necessary for an adult bathtub, but is great for children who can get really dirty. After you bathe your children, rinse the washcloth, add a little soap, then wipe around the tub so there is no dirt or soap scum build up.

➤ **Wipe around the baseboards in your bathroom to pick up any dust or hair with a dirty washcloth, towel, or even clothes from your hamper.** Socks are also great for this.

Bedrooms

➤ **Make up your bed first thing in the morning.** Your bed is a large part of your room, and it will look much neater with the bed made. It also starts you off feeling like you have accomplished something towards keeping a cleaner home. My husband and I use the rule that the last one out of the bed has to make it up. (I love this rule because I am an early riser.) Making up the bed first thing in the morning is also a great habit to get your children into at an early age. Even if they cannot make up their beds to your liking, at least they are going through the motions and will improve their skills as they get older.

➤ **Each week, schedule a bedroom for an "organizational" cleaning.** This means that each room gets special attention about once a month. This is when you really evaluate what is in that particular room and purge items that are outgrown, broken, no longer wanted, or just do not belong. Make a "donate" pile, a "to-sell or consign" pile, and a "trash" pile. For your children's room, sort the items with them and then organize the toys, books, and clothes that they want to keep. This keeps the clutter down, and children tend to enjoy this time with you in their room. When you do it once a month or so, it is not too overwhelming for your child or you. Do not forget about the master bedroom, which needs "organizational" cleaning too. It is not as intense as a child's room, but you still need to purge the never-worn clothes, old socks and t-shirts, magazines that are outdated, etc.

➤ **Clear out anything that is under your children's beds on a weekly basis.** We all know kids love to clean up by shoving everything under their bed. Pick a day to set aside some time to check under their beds and make sure your children clear out all of the mess that may be shoved under there. We have found Sundays to be a good day to do this. Going through this process helps them to quickly understand that they will have to put away the toys and dirty clothes eventually, and that they are not getting away with anything.

Living areas

➤ **Make "toy boundaries."** If your children have ample space in their rooms to play and are old enough to play on their own, feel free to not allow other living spaces to be taken over by toys. Allow maybe one or two toys out at once, and then ensure they are put back in their place once your children are finished playing with them. Your house is a home, and not a toy store. Your limits will vary depending on the age of your children. If your children are at a young age, you can use a decorative basket to keep some toys neatly tucked away, yet accessible for them to use while you cook, make a phone call, etc. As they age, this will not be as necessary and you can adjust your limits.

➤ **A coffee table is not always necessary.** If you have very young children, you may not even want a coffee table in your family room. They are potentially very dangerous for babies learning to pull up or walk. Many of the visits to emergency rooms are attributed to coffee tables. If you can avoid this item in your living space, it will be safer and less to clean. You also pick up a little extra floor space to play on with your children. If you do use a table, keep the items on it to a minimum. Coffee tables tend to be clutter magnets, so you might as well start off with little on it.

➤ **Dust your lamp shades with a lint brush.** This is a quick and effective way to keep your shades dust-free.

Recruiting help from your family

Teaching your children and your spouse how they can help around the house is well worth your time and energy. At an early age your children should learn that doing their part is expected and a necessary component to keeping the home clean and organized.

Some parents neglect to teach their children how to accomplish certain household tasks because it takes time and they believe that they will do a better job anyway. Do not fall into this trap. Whatever time you spend showing a child how to do something will be returned back to you tenfold as the child develops his skills. This will not only help keep your house together, but it develops a child's confidence because he knows he is capable of doing things and has the responsibility to do so.

Some parents also underestimate what children can do.

Children are way more capable than most people give them credit for. It is important, however, to take the time to teach your children exactly what is expected and how to complete the required task. Once you have taught your children how to do each task, follow up to ensure they are doing what is expected. Be careful, however, and do not redo what they have done or they will quickly lose their enthusiasm and confidence in completing what you request. Consider your children's ages and what is reasonable to expect from them. If you can tell they did their best at making up their beds, even if it is not up to your standard, then you should be at peace with that.

▶ **Make a chore list.** Creating a simple chart listing what each family member is responsible for helps to remind everyone of what is expected. I like to write out our chart on the family calendar for all to see. Please note that these chores are above and beyond what is expected from everyone on a daily basis. For example, I do not write down "make your bed" because it is a known fact in our house that each person is responsible for making his bed right when he wakes up. The same is true for clearing the table after supper. What I do write down are the chores such as sweeping the porch or watering the plants. To give you a better idea, an example of our chores list is as follows:

Billy — unload dishwasher, clean the glass doors
Jack — water the plants, help fold the laundry
Jamie — sweep the porches, dust the furniture
Joel Thomas — set the napkins and forks on the table, help switch out the laundry.

Notice that the tasks became easier as I went down the list due to the ages of my children. For my three-year-old, placing napkins and forks on the table before supper is a simple yet age-appropriate task. It also makes him feel like a big boy because he is helping out just like his older brothers and it gets him into the habit of helping.

On the other hand, my nine-year-old is quite capable of unloading the dishwasher. You will know what the age-appropriate chores for your children will be and can adjust them as they age and their skills improve. It is also helpful to switch around the chores so they do not get bored and are able to learn new skills.

Some of the basic chores you should expect your children to do on a daily basis can include the following:

➤ Make your bed every morning before breakfast.
➤ Clear your plate off the table after every meal and snack.
➤ If you spill it, you help to clean it up.
➤ Help set the table.
➤ Bring down your dirty laundry.
➤ Put away the clothes in your clothes basket.
➤ Pick up all of your toys outside before you come in for the day.
➤ Clean up all of your toys in the house after you have finished playing with them.
➤ Pick up your room at night before bed.

➤ **Hold your children accountable**. In order to make any system effective for your family, you have to follow up and hold everyone accountable for what he is responsible for. If your children know that you are going to check to ensure that they in fact did what was required and that they did it to the best of their ability, they will be more likely to do it and do it correctly the first time.

I was having trouble enforcing the "make your bed before breakfast" rule until I created an effective consequence for them. Ideally you could just check their rooms before they sat down to eat breakfast, and if they have not made it, then they do not eat. That seems pretty simple. In our house of four boys, however, it did not always work that way so I decided to check their rooms after their dad took them to school. If I checked and their bed was not made, then when they got home from school they had to not only makeup their bed before they got to eat a snack but they also owed me an additional chore. This worked like a dream!

You can also decide what is important to your children and withhold a certain toy or activity for an allotted amount of time if they do not complete their chores as expected. You can also require that their chores be completed before they get to do a certain activity such as going outside, playing on the computer, or watching television.

➤ **Create incentive programs to help motivate your children.** There are certain ways you can help to motivate your children. Some parents believe that children should be able to keep their rooms the way they see fit and do not hold a very high standard as to what the room should look like. I do believe that a child's room is his room and that he does have some control over its appearance. However, I do have my standards that need to be met for me to consider it acceptable.

I created an incentive program for my children to keep their rooms clean without me constantly reminding them or taking control over their private space. I simply told them that throughout the week I would inspect their rooms in the mornings and whoever kept their room picked up would receive $2.00 at the end of the week. If they chose not to clean it, I did not complain; they just did not get the $2.00. This system was a wonderful discovery and has made both my children as well as myself very happy because we have clean rooms and they get easy money.

For me, it is well worth the money that they earn. You can adjust the amount to fit your family, but when compared to the cost of a housekeeper or being frustrated at the appearance of your children's rooms, I find the money spent to be a fair deal.

➤ **Let your children work for extra spending money.** Most children like to earn extra spending money, which you can use to your advantage. Children should not get paid for work they are expected to do as being a part of the family, but rather chores that are above and beyond their normal duties. Some of these extra chores could be washing the car, scrubbing the railings or columns on the porch, reorganizing a drawer or the pantry, wiping down the kitchen cabinets, etc.

Make a list of chores that you are willing to pay for, so when your children are ready to work for some extra cash, you are ready with tasks that you want accomplished. You can even go ahead and list the payment for each chore so your children are aware in advance of what they are working for. Make sure your children know that if the job is not done to the best of their ability, they are not guaranteed payment. I only pay for the amount of effort they put into the job.

➤ **Use cleaning as a form of consequence for bad behavior.** When timeouts have lost their effectiveness, try having your children do chores instead. As children age, timeouts are not that big of a deal, but having them do chores as punishment may prove to be effective in changing their behavior. It is also a big help to you as well as an opportunity to teach your children a new task.

Our home hit a new level of order and cleanliness when I implemented this concept. And no, it does not make children view housework as punishment. Occasionally, my children would be doing a certain chore and actually enjoy it, and then do more than what was required. I have not seen any negative effects on their attitudes towards cleaning because of this rule. In fact, their views on housework have improved through this system.

It also makes children realize the effects their actions have on the house when they have to scrub the wall they dirtied when they rubbed their filthy fingers on it. This is far more effective than just telling a child to keep his dirty hands off the walls. He needs to see it and then to clean it for it to hit home. If your child deliberately flicks a piece of cereal onto the floor at breakfast, not only should he pick it up, but he should sweep the entire kitchen as well. Doing this helps your children learn to be accountable for their actions, and it shows them what it takes to keep up a house.

If you have two children who are fighting, have them complete a task together to encourage them to make up and work through their conflict. Working together helps them to realize that they are a team and not enemies.

➤ **Decide how your spouse can help you the most.** If you have a spouse that helps you out all of the time without being asked, then you are one of the lucky few. For most other moms, this is a challenging area. Be thoughtful and realistic when thinking about what you really need from your spouse. Consider both of your workloads and the time constraints that you have. If you both work outside of the home, then he should do more than if you are a stay-at-home-mom. Share the responsibilities accordingly.

First, sit down with your spouse and find out what tasks he does not mind doing, and write those down. Some men like folding clothes, while others find sweeping to be an easy chore. Let him do whatever it is that he likes the best. You are looking for help any way you can get it, and any of the chores taken off your to-do list is helpful. Agree that he is responsible for those items and leave it at that. No more nagging! If he committed to doing certain tasks, he is responsible for doing them.

Also, keep in mind, that if he is not perfect at the given task, do not correct him harshly. You will kill any motivation he will have to do it again if you insult his effort and then do it over to make it to your satisfaction. Allow him time to perfect whatever it is he has agreed to do.

Second, keep a master to-do list for your husband of the chores or projects that he is typically responsible for. When you do this, your spouse can easily refer to what needs to be accomplished and you do not have to keep reminding him of all that needs to be done. This goes back to the "no more nagging" rule. Keep the list where it is easily in view, yet not in a place too prominent that it loses its effectiveness. When your spouse has the time to work on a project, he can just go down the list and do what he is in the mood to do and what his times allows for. You can just add to it as projects come up and cross off what has been taken care of.

When all else fails, hire help! If implementing these two suggestions does not prove to be effective in recruiting help and you are still working yourself ragged, inform your spouse that if he is not willing to help you out, then you need to hire someone who will. It is impossible to do everything on your own without paying the consequences over time and some-times hiring a housekeeper to help out can save your sanity.

If you are on a tight budget, decide where you can cut corners to pay for help. The money you spend can be well worth it if you find someone good at a reasonable rate. Ask people you know if they can recommend a housekeeper who can help you out. There are many maid services listed on the internet and in the phonebook, but I have found them to be much higher in cost. Check everything out before you make a decision so you know you made the right one. You can interview several housekeepers to find one that is a good match for your family.

You may only need someone to help you get through a tough period, and then once things let up, you can let her go. After the birth of a baby is a perfect time to bring someone in to clean, even if it is once every two weeks. Anything will give you some relief from the constant duties of keeping up with your house.

Even if you are able to take care of everything in the house on your own, it is good for your children to see your spouse pitching in too. Your children learn from watching you both, and they should see that keeping up with the house is everyone's responsibility. They do not need to grow up thinking that mom is supposed to do everything by herself.

3

Organizing and Keeping up with Your Family's Life

NOW THAT YOU HAVE ORGANIZED YOUR HOME, IT IS TIME TO organize your family. It is natural to think that the larger your family is, the more disorganized you will be, but that is not the case. I have known mothers with only one child who could not keep it together as well as a family with three or four children. It is not about how many children you have, but rather, it is about the systems you are using to stay organized and keep the household running smoothly.

Your family relies on you to be great at making sure everyone stays organized and on top of all of the activities and commitments your family takes on. This ranges from play-dates, doctor appointments, and school events to baseball games or gymnastics. In today's world, life goes much faster and there is much more to do, so being an expert family manager is more important than ever.

If you only have one child and think you do not need to apply the techniques I will describe, you may want to reconsider. Your home will run much more smoothly if there is a system in place to keep your family organized. If your family grows, you will already have created good habits, so it will make having multiple children even that much easier.

Utilizing a day planner

I cannot say enough good things about the use of a day planner. It is a small calendar binder that keeps your whole family together. If you use it the way it is intended, much of your disorganization will be cured. I have been addicted to my day planner since college and have been using it faithfully ever since.

There are different kinds available now, and you will need to look around to find the one that suits you best. I started out with the original Franklin Day Planner and cannot imagine switching to anything else. You may prefer the electronic versions of a planner, or a PDA. Choose whichever style you are comfortable with and one you know you will use. When you are deciding which type of planner to get, I recommend that you choose one that has the following:

> ➤ A "month-at-a-glance" page. This is when you can see the entire month laid out on one page.
> ➤ One or two pages for each calendar day to note your daily tasks, appointments, etc.
> ➤ Address book.

➤ Advance planning calendar for the future year(s).

➤ Pages set up for key information such as important dates to remember, like birthdays and anniversaries.

➤ Goal setting sheets.

➤ Extra numbered tabs and blank lined papers to use as you need.

➤ Side pockets to store important papers. Try to get one that has a zipper to keep papers from falling out.

➤ A page-finder so you can quickly go to the current day.

Once you have purchased a day planner of your liking, give yourself a chance to become familiar with its lay out.Write down all the information that you know at the time, including what activities, appointments, and events your family has lined up. You should be able to open up your planner and know exactly who is supposed to be where at any given moment. Other information can be kept in your planner depending on your needs and lifestyle. Listed below are some of the items I have found very useful to keep in my planner to give you an idea of what your planner can be used for:

➤ Family birthdays and anniversaries.

➤ Addresses.

➤ Listed menus for family meals. (See Chapter 5, "How to Feed Your Family")

➤ When planning a party, designate a section in the back to keep everything you need to prepare for the event. (See Chapter 8, "Entertaining, Birthdays, and Holidays")

➤ Goals for the day, month, week, year, and long-term goals.

➤ Record the days you exercise and your weight.

➤ Whenever you are researching anything, from finding a

good sitter to a swim instructor, designate a section to keep all of the information for easy reference.

➤ Dedicate a page for gift ideas for your friends and family. Whenever you hear someone say they want or need something, jot it down on this page to purchase later.

➤ List all of the gifts you buy for people for holidays and birthdays on its own separate page. Also include the amount you paid so you can keep up with how much you spend.

➤ State goals that you have and your strategies to obtain them.

Keep your planner accessible so you can add appointments and other information as well as being able to reference it whenever you need to. My planner is always within reach because I use it throughout the entire day. It will not be effective for you if you do not put it to use. It may take a little while to get into the habit of using your planner the correct way, but once you see how it can organize your life, you will be hooked.

Be efficient with your time

You need to be the master of your schedule, and to do that, you have to be intentional in all that you do concerning appointments, commitments, and even trips to the store. If you do not have a game plan for your day or your week, you will find yourself wasting valuable time and exerting more energy than necessary. Follow these suggestions to make the most of the little time that busy moms have:

➤ **Schedule appointments to fit your calendar.** Do not

schedule an appointment that suits your dentist if it will not fit into what you have to do that day. Find a time and a day that works for your schedule so that you can be efficient with what you do. Think about what you have to do and how much time you will have. If you drop off the kids and then can make an appointment immediately afterwards, perfect. That is much better than dropping off the kids and then going home for 45 minutes just to have to leave again to make it to the dentist. You will have extra travel time and it splits up your day too much. Make sure you have big chunks of time in your day to do what you need to, not small intervals where you cannot gain any momentum.

➤ **Make the most of your downtime.** Try your best to avoid downtime in your day. By this, I am referring to when you are in your car and do not have enough time to run an errand but have some time to kill before your scheduled appointment or pick-up at school, etc. Sometimes that downtime is unavoidable so keep a magazine, catalogs, a book you may be reading, or the newspaper to read while you wait. By doing this you are not wasting time and you can catch up on some reading that you rarely get to. Also use this time to go through your planner and get organized by checking your calendar and making your to-do lists. This can also be done when you are in a waiting room, the car line at school, or at the salon. Why read the magazines that you do not really care about while you wait when you can bring your own or go through your day planner? Some people do not think about little things like this, but these little things are what help you stay on top of your family's busy life.

➤ **Try not to schedule anything on Mondays.** When you are

scheduling appointments or committing to be somewhere at a specific time, do NOT do it on a Monday. It took a long time before I figured this one out but once I did it helped me out tremendously. Mondays are usually crazy as it is and the house tends to need a little extra attention. This is not the day to add a commitment that can be scheduled on another day. Put things in your favor by keeping Mondays open so you can catch up with the laundry or other housework. This is also very true for the Monday after you return from a vacation.

➤ **Create a time table for your busiest days.** If you have a day that is packed with places to be and things to do, use your planner to help you through it. With four children, this comes up for me a great deal. I have learned how to be where I need to and get it all done with minimal stress by using this tool. I have listed my schedule for a particular day below so that you may see how thinking through what it is you need to do ahead of time can help you through those action-packed days.

8:10 a.m. — Leave with J.T. Take Easter basket & sandwiches
8:45–10:00 a.m. — J.T.'s egg hunt
10:00 a.m. — Leave egg hunt
10:45 a.m. — Arrive at appointment
12:15 p.m. — Have to leave by this time
12:30 p.m. — Arrive at school to volunteer
1:40 p.m. — Leave school for doctor's appointment
2:00 p.m. — Doctor appointment
2:45 p.m. — Pick up at school
4:30 p.m. — Leave the house for soccer
5:00 p.m. — Be at soccer field
5:45 p.m. — Leave soccer field to go to baseball
6:00 p.m. — Be at baseball field

Notice that I wrote down leave times as well as arrival times. This is important to do, because when children are involved you have to add a little cushion to make sure you make it to where you need to be.

On this particular day I actually made it to everything and was able to keep a smile on my face. If I ended up being five minutes late here or there, it was okay because I knew that I was doing the best I could, and it was amazing that I was even there from the start. I could have never done it if I was not thoughtful about the day and had not written down my time schedule. I experienced far less stress than if I had just "winged it" and was constantly estimating in my head when I should leave and how long it would take me to get from here to there. I thought it all through once at home, wrote it down, and then that day I simply had to read my schedule and do what it said. It was as simple as that.

The schedule that I had to keep that day is not something you want to do all of the time, but sometimes it is unavoidable and you have to make the best of it. Utilizing your day planner is a great way to help you through such overbooked days.

Create a family calendar

Purchasing a dry erase calendar board for your family is a must for communicating everyone's activities. Determine the best place to hang one, whether it is in your laundry room, mud room, or on the back door of the pantry. Wherever you place yours, make it easily visible to your family. The size you need will depend on the size of your family and the amount of activities your family participates in.

➤ **Get everyone in the habit of checking the family calendar.** This system is effective in letting your whole family know what is going on with other family members as well as themselves. Everyone can take a glimpse at the calendar the night before and as they head out the door in the morning and be up to date with the day's activities. Teach your children to use this calendar so they become responsible for knowing what they are scheduled to do. By doing so, you are not only teaching them to be responsible for their lives, but you are giving them the gift of organization. The odds are high that they will use the "calendar" system in life to help stay organized as they get older. This will help them to succeed and lead a less stressful life down the road.

➤ **Use a different color marker for each family member's activities.** You could have the color be the same as the cup color your child uses as suggested in Chapter 2, so it is easily identifiable to the whole family. You may also prefer using a certain color for specific activities. For example, all school-related events can be in green, all baseball games in red, all doctor appointments in black, etc. Decide which method might work best for your family and then teach everyone how to read the board.

➤ **Use the family calendar to list which chores each child has for the week and whose room is scheduled for its "organizational" cleaning.** This is referenced in Chapter 2 on keeping your home clean. There is no debate as to who is responsible for what when it is noted on your board. You may want to note whose turn it is to feed the dog, clean out the litter box, clean up after dinner, etc. By doing so, you will prevent arguments of who did what and when and whose turn it is now.

Decide what will be helpful to your family and incorporate it into your family calendar.

➤ **Note major school tests or projects.** Write down upcoming tests that your children have so there are no "surprises" on the day or night before a major test. This will help everyone learn to study ahead and take the pressure off the night before a test is scheduled. Major projects that are due are great to record on the calendar as well. For children who do not have a day planner, this helps them to see how much time they have before a project is due.

➤ **Personalize your family calendar to meet your family's needs.** At my children's school they have a P.E. uniform, a dress uniform and then a regular uniform, all of which get worn in one week. To make it even more complicated, each child has different days in which they are to wear the different uniforms. With all of my children, several people have asked how I can keep straight who is to wear what. It has never been a problem at our house because my husband came up with the great idea of listing at the bottom of the dry erase board the name of the child and which uniform is to be worn under each day. It works like a dream and no one has gone to school wearing the wrong outfit. This is an example of how you can use your family calendar to meet the specific needs of your family.

➤ **Incorporate your day planner with your family calendar.** When you get a list of events, such as a practice or game schedule, or make an appointment, immediately record it on your day planner and on your family calendar. The family calendar, when used in conjunction with your day planner, will keep you organized, and you will never miss an appointment or be confused as to what is going on in your family's life. This will greatly reduce your stress level as well as that of your family's.

Keeping up with schoolwork

➤ **Use your family calendar to keep up with tests and projects.** Even if your children are young and do not have homework yet, there are still school-related issues that need to be organized. Before I had my family calendar and my first child was in preschool, I had a hard time keeping up with which color shirt he was supposed to wear to coincide with the color they were studying at the time or when he was supposed to bring in certain items. It was not homework, but it was something that I was expected to remember. Once I stopped relying on my memory and started keeping up with all of the school-related issues on a family calendar my life became easier. No matter what your children's ages are, the family calendar is a great way to keep schoolwork and/or preschool related issues organized. The family calendar is not a place for daily homework, of course, but rather for major tests, projects, scheduled field trips, show and tell, etc.

➤ **Establish a homework routine.** Once your children are at the homework age, getting everyone into good habits is crucial. Habits that you start early will keep you all organized and help your children's grades as well as your sanity. Every home has a different schedule, so you need to find what works best for your family. If your child comes home right after school, try to get into a homework routine that works. I have found that having a snack and then completing homework immediately afterwards is very effective. I have tried several ways to get homework completed in a timely and positive manner, and this method was the winner. Doing it after supper did not work because the kids were too tired and so were my husband and I. Letting them play before we opened the books also had drawbacks because they dragged out the homework and had no real incentive to do it in a timely manner.

I decided to start the rule that after they had their after-school snack, all homework had to be completed before they could play. Understanding that they could not go outside until their homework was complete and done in a satisfactory manner, they quit wasting time and began doing their homework neatly and quickly. It was so nice to not have to say "finish your homework" about 50 times a day. It definitely improved our homework experience.

➤ **Studying for tests**. Have your children study for tests after they have completed their homework and then quiz them on the material after supper. After supper is not the time to start studying for a test that is to be taken the next day, but a great time to review for it. Use this time to also study ahead for tests. This will take the stress off the night before a test and will improve your children's grades.

➤ **If you have a younger child that loves to serve as the "distractor" during homework time, you have to get creative to keep your little one occupied**. Try giving him a coloring book or blank sheets of paper and crayons to color. If he is old enough, you might want to purchase preschool workbooks so he can work on "homework" just like his older sibling. Pull out puzzles for him to put together, Lego's or any other toy that your child enjoys. Try creating his own homework box that contains items to play with that he only gets to use while his older siblings work on their homework. This box could include Play-Doh, scissors, old magazines to cut out, glue, and other craft material. The point is not to ignore the younger child, but to give him something to do that he will enjoy. He may still run by and swipe the pencil that his sibling is working with just to get a reaction, but if you make it very clear that it is not acceptable and redirect him to his own project, you should have great success. As a bonus, you are also getting your younger child into the routine of doing his homework after snack so it will be a smooth adjustment when he really does have schoolwork to do.

➤ **Stay involved with your children's school work even if it is completed at their school's after-care program.** After-school care is more and more common for single and dual working parents, and many programs have the children complete their homework during this time. If this is the case for your family, I suggest you still stay aware of what your children are working on as well as help them to study for tests. Even if all work is completed in school, your children need to know that you are interested in what they are studying and that their schoolwork is important to you. Designate a time after you get home for you and your children to review what they have been doing, look over returned or graded papers and study for tests. Try not to make this time at the very end of the night when everyone is tired, as it can easily get skipped or not be given the attention it deserves. Realize that this is quality time with your children as well as staying abreast of what they are doing in school.

➤ **Have a quick turnaround on all papers and permission**

slips to be signed. When your children hand you forms to be filled out and papers to be signed, take care of them immediately! Do not stack them on the counter to look at later where they can easily get lost or forgotten. Sign and review their schoolwork, fill out forms, or write checks for fieldtrips, etc., and then put it right back in their book bags. I have read that some people suggest having a binder to store these types of items to be taken care of later. I do not see the point when you can just take care of it right then and there and be done with it. Rarely do you ever have more time later to do anything. Whatever you can take care of now, do it!

➤ **Ask your children to pack up all of their schoolbooks and papers at night**. If you do this, in the morning all they need to do is grab their bags on the way out the door. The morning is not the time to write a note to the teacher or sign papers for your child. Have everything 100 percent completed at night, and your mornings will not only go much more smoothly, but the chance that something is forgotten is greatly reduced. Remember that everything you are teaching your children now about being organized with their schoolwork and studying habits will stick with them all the way through college. It may take extra effort to enforce new habits, but do not get discouraged because it will pay off. Your children need you to help them learn better habits about how to stay organized with their schoolwork.

Balancing extracurricular activities

Nowadays there are so many organized sports and activities to choose from, it can be overwhelming when trying to decide what your children should participate in. Almost all of the offerings available seem as though they would be fun and beneficial to your children, but you have to decide how much you want them to do in order to keep your family's life in balance. Your children would probably enjoy them all; however, you have to help your children choose what they are truly interested in. You do not want to over-commit and end up making everyone miserable because you are overbooked and have no down time. This is very common problem in today's families.

➤ **How do you choose which activities are best suited for your children?** Take cues from your children when deciding what you would think they would enjoy. Of course, if your children are older, they will tell you what they want to do, but it is not so simple when they are young. You should know your children and have a good inclination as to what is likely to be of interest to them.

For example, we were very active in a church where the children's choir was a popular program. All of our friends kept pushing for us to sign up our oldest child. I knew without a doubt that my son did not want to participate by knowing his personality. I finally discussed it with him after my friends kept insisting he would love it. He was five at the time, and I thought maybe I was assuming too much and should give him the chance to decide. Maybe I was wrong to think he was not interested. When I asked him, he looked at me as if he had seen a ghost and made it clear that he had no interest in it whatsoever. I discovered that, yes, I did in fact know my son as I thought I did.

On the flip side, when this same child, who was not yet four years old, played tee-ball for the first time, he was too shy to run the bases. He would clobber the ball off the tee but would not run unless I ran around the bases with him. I did this until he was comfortable, and then he finally started to run on his own. Again, I knew my child and knew he had an intense passion for baseball, even at his young age, and really wanted to be out there. I helped him through his anxiety about it, and to this day he loves the game and is an amazing player. He also gets a good laugh when I tell this story.

I would not have pushed him as much in a sport he did not care about, just as I did not push him to sign up for the church choir. This is not to say that you can be wrong or that your child may want to try something you would have never guessed. This just means you understand who your child is and what his likes seem to be. You have to make choices about what to do and what not to do, and this helps get your started in the right direction.

Reevaluate your children's passion for each activity before committing to it again. See how your children are enjoying the activity and whether they are benefiting from it when it is time to sign up again. Do not assume that they must participate in the same thing every time. They may want to try something new. However, if they are passionate about something, always plan on keeping them active in that area just as long as they do not burn out on it. If one of your children loves tennis, stick with it, but maybe mix it up a little by switching from clinics to private instruction or vice versa. You could consider letting him take a break one semester and having him try something new. You know your child and will know when he needs a change or a break from an activity.

It is helpful for you as a parent to be aware and acknowledge when your child has a true gift in a certain area. If you discover that one of your children has a natural gift, encourage him to reach his fullest potential by staying active in that area. Children can get easily distracted and want to hop from one activity to another. It is great to try out new things, but also continue to encourage your child to develop the gift that he has been given. He will thank you later!

➤ **Remember, do not over-commit!** Whatever you and your children decide to participate in, just please do not over do it. Children need down time too, just like adults. Running your children from one activity to another seven days a week will take its toll on them and your whole family. It is good for children to be bored sometimes and just play like kids. Everything they do does not have to be part of an organized program.

Yes, all four of my children do participate in sports, but I limit them to activities that they really love and do not sign them up for things just to do it. You have to take into account how the schedule of each activity will affect your family. If you are organized with your schedule, it will allow your children the ability to be involved in the activities they love without taxing the family as a whole.

Take the stress out of vacations

It is known that taking a vacation is considered to be one of the more stressful things you can do. It should not be that way, but sometimes all of the preparations and disruptions of a vacation can take a toll on a family. The goal is to eliminate some of that stress so that you and your family can get the most out of your vacation. This is yet another situation where your day planner and being organized is critical.

Designate a section or a page in your planner for your vacations. Here you can keep any information you have concerning your upcoming trip. It is great for when you are researching your vacation destination as well as for recording the final particulars such as flight numbers, hotel confirmation numbers, car rental information, etc. This will enable you to quickly find what you need without having to search for any of your information pertaining to your trip.

Once you have planned the details out for your vacation, you should make two lists. The first list should contain everything you need to do before you leave, and the second should be a list of everything you need to pack for your trip. These lists can be kept in your day planner and used every time you go out of town. Obviously, you will have to make some adjustments as to what you pack depending on your destination but the basics will remain the same.

The first list of what you need to do before you leave for your vacation can be broken down into several time phases. The more you can do ahead of time, the less stress there will be on you and your family. The first list you compile should look something like this:

Weeks ahead of departure

➤ **Pet care.** Coordinate someone to take care of the pets or reserve space for them at a kennel.

➤ **Housesitter**. Coordinate someone to water the plants and check on the house.

➤ **Mail**. Call the post office to stop the mail or ask someone to collect it for you.

➤ **Newspaper**. Call the courier to hold your newspaper while you are away.

➤ **Pay bills**. Make sure all of the bills are paid that will be due while you are away.

➤ **Postage and addresses**. If you are planning to send postcards, have the addresses of the recipients and the postage you will need.

➤ **Keep the day after you return from your vacation clear of any commitments**. Make sure you do not have any appointments scheduled for the Monday after a weekend trip or whichever the next day is after you return. Keep that first full day back free to unpack, get settled, and recharge for the week.

➤ **Decide what outfits you will need to take**. If your trip requires dressier outfits, make sure you have thought out what it is you are going to wear. Allow yourself this extra time to shop if you need to buy something special for the trip.

➤ **Take in your dry cleaning**. If something needs to be dry cleaned, make sure you take it well in advance so you know that your clothes will be ready when you need them.

Several days before departure

➤ **Contact your neighbors.** Alert your neighbors of your absence so they can keep an extra eye on your home.

➤ **Cut the grass.** Do the necessary yard work to maintain the appearance of your home. This is for aesthetics as well as for security. If your grass is overgrown, it can be a signal to potential burglars that you are out of town.

➤ **Deep clean your house.** Cleaning your home before you leave is extremely helpful for you upon your return. If you cannot squeeze in the extra time you need to clean, consider having a cleaning service help you out. You will be so thankful to return to a clean home that it is worth whatever it takes to get it looking right before you leave. This is especially true when you take a longer trip.

➤ **Pack as much as you can ahead of time.** Most of the items you will be taking on your vacation can be packed in advance. Pack as much as you can several days before you are scheduled to leave. Refer to your "packing list" (explained later) and check off what you have in the suitcase as you pack it. This way you do not have to rely on memory when finishing the job the day before leaving.

➤ **If your children are old enough, have them pack their own items.** Tell your children exactly what they need to pack. You should make it very clear such as, "You need to pack four shirts, four shorts, two pajamas, a bathing suit, four pairs of underwear, and four pairs of socks." This gives them a specific instruction that helps them manage the task. Once your children have pulled together the clothes they need, inspect them together to ensure they have everything and then pack them in the suitcase.

➤ **Pack some clothes as you fold them from the dryer.** I have found it useful to pack some of the clothes as I am folding them from the dryer a couple of days before we leave. If you have the counter space, make a pile for each person and stack the necessary items that you know you will take on the trip. Why put it all away in the drawers just to pull it out again to pack it? That goes back to my rule of no double-handling. If your children are packing themselves, they can first check their pile and then add to it the additional items they will need.

➤ **Do not over-pack.** So many people tend to pack more than they need, and it creates extra work and too much luggage. Know what your itinerary is and pack accordingly. Work with your wardrobe and pack pieces that coordinate with each other. Keep a singular color scheme so that the same pair of shoes or the same purse will match everything that you are taking. For example, use brown or black as your base color and then work around it to create different outfits. Pack items that travel well without wrinkling. Also try to choose colors that wear well. You may get two wears out of a dark-colored shirt as compared to a white one. Apply these same principles to your children's clothes as well as your own.

Day of or day before departure

➤ **Complete packing.** Even if you have all of your clothes packed and ready to go, you will have to deal with the last-minute toiletries and medicines, etc. A great time saver for this is to keep your toiletries bag in your bathroom, and then as you use each item the night before and the morning of your departure, you can just toss it in the bag. Another method that works great when packing your toiletries is purchasing duplicates of what you use but in smaller sizes. If you keep travel sizes of your shampoo, conditioner, hair spray, toothpaste, etc., you will not only save time when packing but also in unpacking because you can just leave all of the items in your bag for the next trip. I love this way of handling the bathroom items because it saves so much time and I do not have to worry about forgetting anything. I replace whatever I use up when I return home so it will be there for my next trip.

➤ **Water plants**. If you have plants that are in the direct sun, consider moving them into the shade or at least to an area where there is filtered light. This way they will not require as much water while you are gone. This is helpful if you do not have someone to come by and water your plants or if you will not be gone long enough to bother with coordinating someone to do it. Having the plants in the shade can buy you a couple of days more without water.

➤ **Complete all of your dirty laundry**. Do not leave any dirty laundry in your hampers if you can help it. If you keep up with it in the days before you leave, this will be easy to do and you should only have one last load right before you go.

➤ **Last-minute clean up in the house**. Make sure dirty dishes are washed and your kitchen is clean. Try to put away any miscellaneous items throughout the house so you return to a clean home. This is a good time to use the trick of having your husband load the kids in the car while you do a last run through in the house to get it cleaned.

➤ **Clear the entrance.** If you are not able to do a last-minute pick up in your house, then check out the view from your front door and any other door from which visitors can see the inside of your home. Make sure that from this viewpoint your house does not look messy. This may sound crazy, but it is a great thing to do when you just cannot seem to pick up everything before you leave. When my four children were all under the age of six and we would go on vacation, I discovered this technique. I was able to deep clean the house and pack, but while I was doing that, the boys would be playing with toys to stay occupied. I just could not pick up all the little pieces, and as much as they tried to help me, it was unsuccessful. I learned that if I could just push the toys out of sight from my front door, it was okay. I did not want someone to come by the house and see the messy toys and think that was how the rest of my house looked. I knew it was clean, but the first impression of toys in the foyer would not have convinced anyone. Also, your reentry into your home will be a little better if scattered toys are not the first thing you see when you walk in the door.

➤ **Double-check the house.** After you have loaded the car or taxi to leave, walk through the house to look for those forgotten items that you are supposed to take with you. Many people have been guilty of leaving a garment bag on the bed or a toothbrush by the sink. If you do a final walk through, the odds that you left something behind are greatly reduced.

What to pack

What you need to pack will vary from family to family and vacation to vacation; however there are still some basic items that need to be packed every time. Making a standard list helps to save time and prevents you from forgetting items that you will need. You can keep the list in your day planner or on your computer to print out whenever you need it. Leave space on your list to add the items that are specific to your particular trip.

To get you started on your packing list use the items listed below:

➤ Digital camera with back-up batteries, or a traditional camera with extra film.
➤ Plane tickets and accommodation information
➤ Sunscreen
➤ Sunglasses
➤ Cash and credit cards
➤ Kids' outfits
➤ Kids' pajamas
➤ Kids' shoes
➤ Parents' outfits
➤ Parents' pajamas
➤ Parents' shoes
➤ Bathing suits
➤ Toiletries — shampoo, conditioner, soap, facial products, hair dryer, curling iron, mousse, toothbrushes and toothpaste, makeup, deodorant, shaving cream and razors, hair brush, and hairspray
➤ Addresses and postage for postcards

➤ Books and activities for the children in the car or plane
➤ Medicines
➤ Snacks and water bottles for the trip

While on vacation

Once you are off and officially on vacation, a realistic expectation as to how your trip will play out will improve your enjoyment level by reducing unnecessary stress. Traveling with children definitely changes how you vacation, and realizing this will improve your experience. Try not to push your family too hard by cramming in as many activities as you can.

My family lived in Orlando, Florida for six years and visited Walt Disney World more times than I can remember. While at the theme parks, it was not uncommon to see parents pushing their children to the point at which no one was enjoying himself. The parents were so intent on getting it all in that it became taxing to everyone. Who cares how many rides you get on if everyone is too stressed and exhausted to enjoy them? Understand your children and yourself and know when you are trying to do much and adjust your itinerary accordingly.

Follow these tips to help make your vacation run a little smoother:

➤ **Try to time meals during off times**. Go to lunch at 11 a.m. or 2:30 p.m. instead of right at lunch hour. This greatly reduces the crowds and lines.

➤ **Try to keep your children's eating habits consistent with how you eat at home.** Do not overload them with sugar, fast food, and soft drinks. Many a child has gotten sick while on vacation due to the junk that he has consumed. Keep it healthy.

➤ **Try to keep reasonable bed times.** Just because you are on vacation does not mean you should let your children stay up too late, causing them to be tired and miserable the next day.

➤ **Take needed breaks throughout the day to relax if your day is filled with lots of activities and time constraints.** Just sitting on a park bench enjoying an ice cream cone can give you a little down time and be rejuvenating for your family.

➤ **Have a game plan for your day, but be flexible within it.** If things are not going as you expected when you made your plan, adjust it. Do not be so rigid that it takes the fun out of the trip.

➤ **Ask around to see if anyone you know has been to where you are vacationing and ask for pointers.** Learn from their mistakes and successes to help improve your vacation experience.

While on vacation, there are also a few little things that you can do to help yourself out when you arrive home. You do not want to be consumed with this and have it take away from your vacation experience, but if it works out for you to do just a few things to prep your return home, you may find it helpful.

➤ **If you are staying with a close relative and can do some of your laundry while you are there, take advantage of this.**

This can help you to pack fewer items because you know you can wash them to wear again, and it will reduce the laundry you need to do when you return home.

➤ **If you are staying at a hotel, make use of the plastic laundry bags they usually provide in the closet to put your dirty clothes in.** This is a great way to separate the dirty clothes and keep them from contaminating the clean items you may have in your suitcase.

➤ **If possible, try to have a separate piece of luggage for each person in the house.** This way, when you unload, each bag goes directly to that person's room. That person is responsible for his putting away his own things and there is not a pile of luggage on the family room floor waiting to be unpacked.

➤ **If your family shares suitcases, try to separate the children's clothes from the adults' when you pack to head home.** This way you can put the adult bag in the master bedroom and put the children's bag in a central area to separate each child's clothes so that he can put them away himself. I like to put the clean items and whatever else belongs to each child in his personal baskets in the laundry room for them to put away. You may also try putting all the clean clothes in one bag and all the dirty ones in another. Whichever method works best for you will be determined by how much of each you have as well as how many luggage pieces you take. The goal is to keep the dirty and clean clothes separate as well as make it easy to separate each person's clothes. The thought you put into packing for home will help tremendously when you go to unpack.

Returning from vacation

Now that the fun of your vacation has ended, it is back to the real world. Having a smooth reentry back home can help you savor those wonderful memories you created while away. When we had grown to a family size of six, sometimes we would go out of town for the weekend three times in one month. Through all of our many travels, I have tried many techniques to find the one that worked best. Listed below are a few pointers that should help you get back to your life at home without the stress of feeling overwhelmed by all there is to do:

➤ **Have a clear game plan with your family as to what is going to happen once you pull into the driveway.** Give everyone a task that is age appropriate. Try to give each child the same task each time so that he knows to expect it and is able to master that particular skill. For example, my nine-year-old knows that when we return from vacation it is his job to unpack the cooler. I do not even have to tell him, and he has done it enough that he knows how to do it right. Put one person in charge of running the first load of dirty clothes, or helping to unpack the car or, my favorite, cleaning out the mess that was created in your car while on your travels. Help yourself out by cleaning out your car as soon as possible to improve your mood when you get in it the next day. There's nothing worse than having vacation debris fall out of your car when you are dropping off the kids at school the next day.

➤ **Resist the urge to go through your mail or check your voicemail right when you get home.** You have enough to do without adding this to the list. Wait until everything is unpacked or at least until you are at a good stopping point before you try to go through your mail. The same applies to checking email. If you still have an answering machine, unplug it when you go out of town so you do not have to contend with the missed calls. This keeps people from wondering why you never called them back because they are not able to leave a message and you also do not have to deal with returning all of the calls. If there is a real emergency, you can always be reached on your cell phone.

➤ **The more you can do the day you return the better.** You may not be able to unpack everything, but give it your best shot. Your family's life will pick up right where it left off, leaving you little time to unpack what has not been done immediately. Have the whole family pitch in and get the job done quickly. Everyone likes to be reminded of their wonderful vacation, but not because they keep tripping over the luggage they never unpacked.

Planning a successful move

This topic should have its own chapter. Actually, it should have its own book. Moving, let alone moving with children, can be a very stressful time and should be executed in the most organized manner possible. A great move does not happen by accident. A lot of thought and care needs to be given to this major family event to make it as easy as possible on everyone.

Our family may have moved more than most. In fact, we moved nine times in the first 14 years of our marriage. Some of the moves were within the same community and some were back and forth from Florida to South Carolina. We even had a stretch where we moved every May for five straight years, with three young children for two of the moves and then four children for the last three moves. Please note that this is not because we seek chaos and cannot stay in one place long. Although we do like excitement, it was really because we wanted to take advantage of the rapid appreciation that was occurring in the real estate market. We were also trying to get back home to my native town of Charleston, South Carolina.

Needless to say, through the many moves we made I was able to fine-tune the process as much as possible. By the last move we were settled in with pictures hung and all boxes unpacked after two weeks. Remember, the ages of our children were 8, 6, 5, and 2. This is quite an accomplishment and only happened because we were very organized about the move and put a lot of thought into how it was executed. The points listed below can help make your move be as easy as possible. If you follow them you will experience less stress and your life will return to normal as quickly as possible.

Preparing your family for the move

➤ **Having a positive attitude towards the move is paramount!** One of the most important things that you can do for your family is to have a great attitude about your move. If you are apprehensive and stressed about moving, your children will be too. Even if you have to fake it a little, try to be as positive and enthusiastic as you can. Talk about the excitement of being in a new place and meeting new people. Allow your children to play a very active part in decorating their new rooms, and let them have some fun with it. Make it a big deal for them and allow them to choose the theme for the room, the paint colors, new bedspreads, or other items to be hung on their walls or placed on shelves. This can be a great way to give your children a positive outlet concerning the move. It also helps to take their mind off some of their apprehensions about relocating.

➤ **Explain to your children exactly what is going to take place.** You may think that your children understand what is transpiring, but they may have no idea. I learned this lesson when we discovered that one of our children truly thought that the people who lived in the house we were moving into were going to continue to live there with us. My child had met the owners when we looked at the house during an inspection and he thought we were all going to live together. Who would have ever dreamed that a child would think that was going to happen? You cannot explain it enough to ensure they are very clear about what is going to take place. Needless to say, our child was greatly relieved when we assured him that the previous owner and his family were moving out, along with all of their belongings!

Assure your children that all of their possessions are going to be moving with them. They need to know that just because their stuff is going to be packed away in boxes for a while does not mean that they will never see their things again. This is a big deal for children, so make sure you cover it thoroughly so it is completely understood.

Moving your belongings

➤ **Choose your mover wisely.** To help choose the best mover for your family, research the moving companies in your area and talk to people you know who have used movers. Find out from friends if they would recommend a certain company or if they have used a company that you should avoid. Set up appointments with at least three companies to have them explain what they will do for you and how much it will cost. It is usually best if a company uses its own movers regularly and does not hire out day laborers to get the job done. This helps ensure that the people moving your furniture have plenty of experience and a solid track record with the moving company.

➤ **Decide how much packing you will do.** How much a moving company does for you depends on what you are willing to do yourself. When the moving company's representative is there to give you an estimate, ask him to break down how much it will cost if they pack and unpack your belongings, and then compare that price to the quote on you packing and unpacking. This allows you to analyze what your time is worth to determine which route you want to take.

There are several arrangements you can make with your mover. Listed below are some of the options you may have, along with their advantages and disadvantages.

➤ I have never chosen to have movers unpack my belongings, because all of my friends that have done this said it did not go well for them. Their complaint was that even though you had all of your belongings unpacked, they were laid out all over the kitchen counters and on the floors throughout the house waiting to be attended to. With children in the house it sounded like a nightmare to me and I have chosen to always unpack myself. If you are able to have the children out of the house for a long period of time to allow you to put everything away quickly, maybe this method could work for you. Just be aware that you do not have the luxury to unpack as you see fit; it has to be attended to immediately.

➤ One of the advantages of packing your belongings yourself, besides the obvious cost savings, is that it gives you the opportunity to purge through items that you may not want to move. It is a great way to get to see what you really own and determine what you need to get rid of and what you want to keep.

➤ If you decide you would rather have the movers pack your belongings, try to go through your items and purge what you do not want to move. Designate a room a week and get rid of things that your child has outgrown or toys that have lost their pieces as well as kitchen items that you never use. Do not move items that you do not need. Not only will you pay for the weight that it carries (most, if not all, movers charge you by the actual weight of your belongings), but you will have to unpack it and deal with it at your new home. This task should not take you too long if you have followed the principles stated earlier in this book.

➤ Another alternative is to have the movers pack just the fragile items, like your kitchen dishes, and you pack everything else. It does not have to be all or nothing. Packing clothes into wardrobe boxes is easy and allows you to label exactly what is in each box. It was hard for me to find clothes that I needed when the movers packed them because they were not as detailed in labeling the boxes as I would have been.

➤ You could also have the movers only pack certain rooms.

Having your children help pack their own rooms can be a good experience for them because they are physically a part of the move and can understand better that their things are going to move with them and not be left behind.

➤ **Whatever you pack, make sure to label your boxes clearly.** Each box should state which room it goes into and some detail as to what is in it. Make the room location large and obvious for the movers, and then in smaller print list what is in the box. I have never unpacked a box that I thought I wrote too much description on. It will help you out tremendously when you go to unpack your boxes or if you need to find a certain item before you have had a chance to unpack every box.

➤ **Ask close friends or family members to help you pack and/or unpack.** Throw a packing party and serve drinks and hors d'oeuvres to your helpers. It can be a great way to get a lot accomplished and visit with friends you may be leaving behind.

Once you are settled in your new home

➤ **Try to get involved in your new community as quickly as you can.** This can help your children meet friends and feel a part of their new area much faster. The same holds true for you and your spouse. You will be very busy the first couple of weeks, but try to seek out places to meet people.

➤ **Try to sign up your children in camps at the school they will be attending.** This will not only help them to become familiar with the school's campus, but it also allows them to meet some of their future classmates. The first day of school will be much easier if they are able to feel comfortable at their new school early on.

➤ **Check out other camps that you believe your children would enjoy.** Camps such as vacation Bible schools can be a great choice, especially if you are able to volunteer. You being there with them can help make your child even more comfortable in this new setting. It is also a great way for you to meet new people. Investigate other camps in your area that are offered in an environment you trust.

➤ **Check out the local library for special events or activities.** Any activity offered for children can help smooth the move transition. Libraries have special reading times for children of different ages and can be a great way to meet people as well as an opportunity to get out of the house.

4

Planning for the Day Ahead

OH, THE MORNING RUSH TO GET OUT THE DOOR! EVERY family goes through the chaos of getting everyone up, fed, dressed, and out the door in as little time as possible. It can make you feel like you are working in a pit crew.

After reading this far in the book, you now have the information you need to take control of the morning circus. I have listed some points that will help you to be ready for the excitement of the morning ahead and turn what used to be a stressful time in your family's day into a pleasant one.

How to get organized the night before

➤ **Have all book bags and equipment for extracurricular activities packed and ready to go by the door.** It does not count if the books are lying next to the book bag; they need to be in the bag with it zipped up and ready. If you have a younger child, put the diaper bag there as well with everything you might need for the next day. You may find it helpful to just leave the diaper bag in the car and replace what items you use as needed. This gives you one less thing to drag back and forth from the house to the car and one less thing you might forget to take.

➤ **Keep the children's shoes by the door.** Have the shoes by the door so no one is searching in the morning for that lost shoe. If you have a child with shoes for every outfit, you obviously cannot keep them all by the door without it looking like a shoe store, so have him pick out the shoes for the next day and put them by his book bag.

➤ **Lay out the clothes for the next day.** The clothes for the next day should be laid out so everyone can get dressed quickly. This includes the parents too. If something needs to be ironed, do it now; do not wait until morning.

If your children have uniforms that they are required to wear for school, you may find it helpful to just keep them hanging or folded in the laundry room. This way, there is no hunting around looking for uniforms if they are not exactly where they are supposed to be. If your children have a specific outfit that they must wear, such as to a baseball game or gymnastics meet, it may be helpful to keep them in the laundry room as well. By keeping them together and in the same location, you always know where they are and that they are clean.

I am embarrassed to admit it, but before I implemented this system I had to send my kids to school with dirty uniform shirts because I did not know they had cleaned up their rooms by shoving their dirty clothes under the bed. They did not have one clean school shirt in the house, and I did not even know it. It was that day that I changed my ways. I was horrified to send them with dirty shirts. Thank goodness the color was a hunter green. I swore it would never happen again, and with my new method of keeping them visible in the laundry room, it never has. I can easily see what is there and notice what is not for the next day of school.

If you choose this system, at night before bedtime have your children take to their room whatever they must wear the next day. This is a guaranteed way to realize if there is something missing. My kids even have fun with it and sometimes make a "person" with their clothes laid out flat on the floor. They position the pants, shirt, underwear, socks and belt so that it looks like a little man. This is a fun and effective way to teach your children to lay out their clothes each night and allows them to see if they have forgotten something. This will also be a habit that, like a lot of others in this book, will carry with your children through adulthood and help set them up for success.

▶ **Have the coffee pot loaded and ready to turn on in the morning, or better yet, purchase one with a delay start so you do not have to do anything the next morning.**

▶ **Prepare for the morning's breakfast.** Know in your mind what is going to be served for breakfast the next day and do any prep work for it the night before. You can even have a set menu for each day of the week that you write out on your family calendar. Knowing what you will serve helps to speed things along and takes the guess work out of the morning rush. You can even put out the nonperishable items on the counter so you, or your children, can quickly get breakfast started.

An example of your week's menu schedule could look like the following:

Monday – oatmeal and fruit
Tuesday – scrambled eggs and grits
Wednesday – pancakes
Thursday – cheese toast and fruit
Friday – cereal

A helpful hint: make a triple batch of pancakes to eat several mornings throughout the week. You can wrap the extras in paper towels and store them in a large re-sealable bag placed in the refrigerator. You can reheat them wrapped in the paper towel for about 15 seconds in the microwave. It makes for a quick and well-received breakfast throughout the week.

➤ **Set the breakfast table at night to save extra time in the morning.**

➤ **Have your personal to-do list planned out so it is obvious what you will need when you head out the door.** This includes dry cleaning, grocery lists, and whatever else you may need to tend to. Have everything together and ready. If you have a lot of things you need to take with you the next day, load the car the night before so you do not have to make multiple trips from the house to the car during the morning rush. This will also help to prevent you from forgetting anything in the morning.

Getting through the morning rush

➤ **Set your alarm early enough to give you and your spouse enough time to be up and ready for the day before your children wake up.** Your family's work and school schedule will determine how your mornings will operate, so take that into consideration when deciding how early you need to get out of bed. It is much easier to manage the children in the morning when you have already gotten yourself ready, so allow for that time. If you cannot be completely ready to head out the door before your children wake up, being even partially ready helps keep things running a little smoother.

➤ **Work as a team with your spouse.** If your husband takes the kids to school before work, allow him to finish getting ready while you are helping to get the children ready and breakfast together. My husband and I alternate mornings, so when I take the children to school, he takes care of most of the morning routine with the kids while I finish getting ready to head out the door, and vice versa. The goal is to get out of the door on time and in a graceful manner, so work together to decide how that is possible for your family.

➤ **If your children are not awake on their own, wake them up by turning on the lights and opening the shades.** A little bit of light really helps get anybody out of bed.

➤ **Wake up the child that is the hardest to get up first, make your rounds to the other children, and then loop back to the first child.** Children have different sleeping needs, just as adults do, so take that into consideration and try to respect how your child likes to get up. If you understand what works best for each child, it will make the morning better for him and you.

➤ **Have your child make up his bed before leaving his room.** This is a wonderful habit to maintain. If the child is very young, you can help him until he is capable of doing it on his own. The bed may not be perfect when they are young, but they will improve their skills eventually, and it gets them into the routine. When the children return home it will give their room a sense of order.

➤ **Have everyone dress completely before they are allowed to eat breakfast.** This rule changed our morning rush dramatically. There is great incentive to get ready quickly when a child knows he does not get to eat until he is dressed and ready for school.

➤ **Be a clock-watcher!** Know when breakfast needs to be finished in order to get out the door on time. Once the clock hits that cut-off time, it is time to finish eating and clean up.

➤ **Have your children clean up their own mess.** Even a three-year-old can load his dishes in an empty dishwasher and throw away his napkin. Again, start good habits now and you and your children will reap the rewards now and later.

➤ **Keep an extra set of toothbrushes and toothpaste for the children in the kitchen if you have a large or two-story home.** This way you can have everyone brush after breakfast without them going far and getting distracted by other things. In addition, when they are young, you can supervise their brushing if you are not doing it yourself. The idea here is to not have them go off on their own and lose focus on trying to get out the door. Implementing this routine in our house cut down on a lot of frustration and lost time.

➤ **Keep a brush and other items you need for your children's hair handy for the morning.** When you have items such a brush and ponytail holders handy, you can quickly make your children's hair presentable without chasing each child from room to room. A bottle mister with water helps keep those bed head mornings at bay, so keep that accessible as well.

➤ **Check your family calendar and go over with everyone what the day's activities will entail.** Even though you went over it the night before, children (and adults for that matter) need to be reminded of what is scheduled for the day ahead.

➤ **Know your load time!** Remember to watch what time you have to start loading and do not start loading when you are supposed to be leaving. We all know that it takes longer to load than we usually allow time for. Also, add some cushion for that last-minute trip back into the house.

➤ **Send everyone off with a hug and a kiss before they head out the door!** Even if your morning did not go as smoothly as you would have liked, always send the family out on a happy note. If you just finished correcting your child for doing something wrong, you should still let him know he is loved and send him off with an "I love you!" This will make your day as well as your children's go a lot better.

5

How to Feed Your Family

ONCE CHILDREN ENTER THE PICTURE IN YOUR LIFE, FOOD AND nutrition take on a whole new meaning. No longer can you skip a meal or two or just grab whatever you can with little thought about nutrition. Starting from pregnancy, the food that you consume is critical to your child's health and development. It is at this time that, if you have not already been conscious of this, you need to respect food for what it is and realize that your food choices directly affect you and your child's overall health.

Eating well for your child during pregnancy is the easy part because you control what foods you consume; it is once the child is born and has a say as to what he eats that complicates things. It is up to you to educate yourself about nutrition and to provide choices for your children that will help them to thrive and protect their health down the road. You are also creating habits that your children will most likely carry with them through the rest of their lives.

In our society where obesity is becoming more and more of a problem and where researchers continue to find the link between unhealthy eating and diseases and illnesses, it is imperative that you make good food choices for you and your family. Life is different now than it was when our grandparents could eat straight off their farms with fresh milk, meat, and vegetables. Companies have created artificial additives and preservatives that prolong shelf-life and supposedly improve the taste or make for better packaging and shipping of the product. We are consuming more chemicals, preservatives, and additives which all have an adverse effect on our health. Food companies have the goal of making money, and it is up to us to educate ourselves about what it is we are consuming. Just because it is on the shelf at the grocery store does not mean it is healthy or even safe for us to eat. Your number-one weapon against this is education.

Making healthy choices

Foods

The recent attention to trans-fats, which mostly come from partially hydrogenated oils, is a perfect example of why it is important to learn about what is in the foods you eat. About 11 years prior to FDA mandating that food manufacturers list the grams of trans-fats on their nutritional information label, I had read that certain groups had researched partially hydrogenated oils and suspected them to have very negative effects on a person's health. The recommendation of the research was to avoid the consumption this ingredient.

I read this information right before I got pregnant with our first child and wanted to protect our unborn baby as much as I could. In an effort to do that I decided to eliminate from my diet all partially hydrogenated oils, as well as other artificial preservatives, food colorings, and other additives I had read negative reports on. The research I had read all suggested that these ingredients had an adverse effect on a person's health and were to be avoided.

I went to the store and read all of the nutritional information labels on items I usually purchased to see if they contained these ingredients. I was stunned and frustrated so much by what I found that I came home in tears. I will never forget crying to my husband saying that there were no safe foods for me to eat because almost every product had an artificial something or other that could harm our baby.

I quickly realized that in order to give my child, as well as myself, a healthy advantage I was going to have to be a smart shopper. I decided to allow to for an extra 15 minutes on my next several shopping trips in order to read the labels of products I normally purchased. This gave me the chance to find the "safe" brands of the products I wanted. Sometimes there were not any that were free of the trans-fats, preservatives such as BHT, BHA and TBHQ, or artificial coloring. In that case I resolved to stop eating those items and find a healthier choice to replace it.

How to choose healthy foods

➤ **Avoid food preservatives such as** BHA, BHT, TBHQ, **and sodium nitrate**. These preservatives are commonly found in cereals, most processed foods, and luncheon meats. Read all of the food labels for these ingredients and avoid them as much as possible.

➤ **Choose your cereal wisely**. The cereal aisle is probably the most challenging to go through. Even the cereals that claim to promote good health and would seem to be a wise choice may have partially hydrogenated oils and preservatives in them. The best choices for cereals are the ones you find in health foods stores or the health aisle at your local grocer. You may find a few of the "mainstream" cereals that are free of additives and preservatives. Due to increased consumer awareness, more and more healthy options are becoming available. Carefully read the labels on the boxes to determine which are safe to consume.

➤ **Just because it says "zero trans fats" does not mean it is safe**. The FDA allows for food manufacturers to claim that their products are "trans fat free" if there is less than 0.5 grams of trans fat per serving. A product may claim this and yet still contain partially hydrogenated oils. The problem here is, first, there is really no safe amount of trans fat consumption. Researchers are still unclear if any consumption is safe. So far, they have told people to consume no more than two grams per day.

Secondly, the serving sizes are so small that rarely do people consume just one serving. Therefore, even if the packaging claims "no trans fats," read the label to see if it contains partially hydrogenated oil. If it does, avoid that product.

➤ **Shop the perimeter of grocery stores.** Shopping the perimeter of a store is an easy way to keep things healthy. This is where you find the fruits, vegetables, dairy, meats, and breads. These are for the most part natural foods and not of the processed variety. Once you have figured out what the good food choices are, your shopping actually becomes easier because many of the items in the store are no longer an option.

Beverages

Beverages should be scrutinized the same way as you would your food intake. The large amount of beverage options available now is amazing. There are many drinks to choose from, so you have to be aware of which ones are doing your body good and which are just filling you and your children up with empty calories. Reading the labels on drinks is your best defense so you know exactly what is going into your body. If a drink contains a lot of calories and has no nutritional value, then you are better off drinking something else.

➤ **Limit your children's sports drink consumption.** In the media right now we are constantly hearing how sedentary our youth has become and that child obesity is becoming epidemic. On the same note, sports drinks are a large part of beverage sales more so now than ever before. Sports drinks were originally created as a drink to consume after or while engaging in strenuous activity. Today's children are drinking sports drinks regularly, regardless of their activity level. They are consuming unnecessary calories, and it is being used to replace other beverages that are good for them.

➤ **Limit, or eliminate, the intake of soft drinks in your family's diet.** Soft drinks are something that also compose a large part of our society's beverage consumption, yet there is no nutritional benefit to them. In fact, studies have shown that they may actually be detrimental to people's health, especially to growing children that need all of the nutrients they can get. This holds true for the regular soft drinks as well as the low-calorie ones. If your family consumes these chemical-laden drinks on a regular basis, you should try to eliminate them from your diet as much as you can. An occasional soft drink here and there is probably fine, but do not buy soft drinks to be consumed regularly in your home.

➤ **Drink plenty of water.** Encourage your children to drink water as a major part of their liquid intake. The benefits of water are plentiful, and water is necessary for your body to operate and thrive properly. Your family will drink more water if you stop buying other unnecessary beverages.

How can you not love water? It is usually free, does not stain your children's lips, clothes, or your carpet, it is not sticky to clean up if it is spilled, does not spoil if left out of the refrigerator, and is what makes up about 75 percent of your body. I read about a dad who gave his children $1.00 each when they ordered water at a restaurant. He said it encouraged them to not drink the soft drinks they would have normally ordered, and it saved him money because of the high cost of the sodas. When my children order water at restaurants, the server always looks shocked and tries to get them to order a soft drink or lemonade. They cannot believe that a child would actually choose to drink water. However, I do admit that my kids love a soda when they can get it, but for the most part they still choose water. (If you have an infant or baby, do not supplement his diet with water until you talk to your pediatrician. In the early part of life there is a delicate balance of breast milk/formula and water that needs to be followed.)

➤ **Cut back or eliminate the "juice boxes."** A lot of people believe that they need all of the juice boxes and other "cool" drink options for their children, when water is still the better alternative. Companies are masters at marketing, so do not be fooled into thinking that their products must be a staple in your home.

Even more important to note is the fact that most juice boxes contain high fructose corn syrup as one of their main ingredients. This ingredient has been linked to an increase in the risk of diabetes and triggers your brain into thinking it is still hungry even if you are full, which can lead to overeating and obesity. Studies have also shown that high fructose corn syrup can raise triglyceride levels in your bloodstream, which can increase the risk of heart disease. Remember, this is the same ingredient that is found in the cute juice boxes and sports drinks that children regularly consume.

Fast food

The foods that you feed your children now will help to develop their tastes and preferences for foods that they will carry with them throughout their lives. If your children are used to fast food and junk food, then they will grow up with a preference for those types of food. It will be harder for them to change their bad eating habits than if you had brought your children up eating healthy foods that are not loaded with fat and salt. Your goal is to ensure your children are getting the proper vitamins and nutrients they need and to limit, if not eliminate, the foods that are unhealthy.

Understand that I do not mean you have to completely forbid your children to eat a little junk once in a while, but make sure they know that it is an exception and not the rule.

Even when you are giving in to junk food, choose the healthier varieties. Buy the chips that are baked and without trans fats, preservatives, or food coloring. And if they eat ice cream, choose the kind that is all natural. Even though natural products may sometimes cost more, it is worth it because they do not contain what I like to call, "all of the bad."

In a society that is always on the go, fast food has become extremely popular for families. Even though it may seem like an easy food option on a busy day, do not fall into the trap of frequenting these establishments because they are not good for you. Even when you choose some of their so called "healthy options," they are still loaded with salt and additives. This is not only true of the fried foods, but even many of the salads and grilled sandwiches that you would consider to be a safe choice. If you ask one of the restaurants you frequent for their nutritional information guide, you will find many of the harmful additives I have discussed. Reading what is in the food you allow your family to consume can be a great motivator to get you out of the habit of buying it.

You may think that eliminating fast food from your diet is next to impossible, but it is easier than you think. It is all about what you are in the habit of doing, and you will be surprised how easy it can be to reduce or even eliminate fast food from your diet all together. Once you stop eating fast food and junk food regularly, it will no longer tempt you as much as it once did because your taste buds will have been adjusted to a healthier diet. Even when you do eat those types of food again, it will probably not be as tasty as you remember it.

➤ **How to avoid the fast food temptation.** Start keeping some nonperishable snacks and water bottles in your car. You can use a plastic container with a lid to store some of your snacks so that you always have something healthy available. This helps to hold you over until you get home to eat a real meal. If you plan ahead, it is easy to avoid the fast food trap. You know that if you are going to pick up your children after school and then go to a practice before you get home, the kids will be hungry, and rightfully so. It is no surprise; you just have to plan for it. Have some crackers, trail mix, or fruit available for your children to eat. You can even pack a little cooler with peanut butter and jelly sandwiches and some grapes that will tide you over until dinner. It may take a little planning and a few extra minutes, but I guarantee that you will spend more time and money at a drive-through if you go to a fast food joint.

Some of you might wonder if children brought up without fast food as a part of their lives will rebel as soon as they get their license and will hit every McDonald's out there. From what I have seen, read, and experienced, that is not the case. The eating habits you establish for your children now will stick with them throughout their lives.

Snacks

Snacks can be a wonderful way to supplement your children's diet if you have healthy options available for them. It is hard for children to get the calories and nutrients they need in just three meals a day, so adding in a snack or two to their diet is important. The old school thought of having three square meals a day has been replaced by the concept of consuming three smaller meals with two snacks in between. Incorporating a healthy snack during the day helps to keep hunger at bay and prevent overeating. It also keeps your metabolism going, which is an important factor in maintaining a healthy weight.

The key is to remember that the word "snack" is not synonymous with "junk." You need to be smart about the snacks you provide to get the biggest benefit from them. You also do not want your children to eat so much that they ruin their next major meal. Your children's age and whether or not they are in school will determine how much they eat and when. Setting some structure to how your children snack will help you to accomplish what you want from this additional meal time.

▶ **Establish times when it is appropriate to eat a snack.** When your children were babies, you most likely had a feeding schedule for them that you used as a guide. This same mentality should continue even when they are old enough to fix their own snack. Make a rule as to the time snacks are allowed in your house and stick to it. This will prevent you from being in the kitchen all day preparing food and cleaning up each time your children have the slightest hunger pang. It will also teach your children better eating habits.

An example of a possible meal and snack schedule is as follows:

7:00 a.m. — breakfast
10:00 a.m. — snack
12:30 p.m. — lunch

3:00 p.m. — snack
6:00 p.m. — supper

This works well for our family and we are a little flexible when schedules are different due to various activities. It gives us a guideline to follow and prevents the children from coming in and out of the kitchen in the constant search for food. I used to be less strict about this and found that all I did was feed one of the kids and then clean up just to have someone else in the kitchen asking for more food. I lived in the kitchen and it got old fast. It also helped the children understand that the kitchen is not a revolving door and that when it is time to eat, they need to eat. They quickly learned that they were not going to get more food until the next meal or scheduled snack time.

➤ **What is available for snack is something that you and your children can decide together.** Get your children's input about what they like from a list of choices that you come up with. The goal is to find some snacks that your children like and that you feel good about them eating.

Refer to the list below to get ideas for some healthy snack ideas.

- ➤ string cheese
- ➤ applesauce
- ➤ yogurt
- ➤ trail mix
- ➤ nuts (if your child is old enough to eat them)
- ➤ apple slices, plain or with peanut butter
- ➤ cut fruit
- ➤ carrot sticks and celery, plain or with dip
- ➤ cheese on baked tortilla chips

➤ homemade muffins (Most store-bought muffins contain too much fat and additives. You can find a few boxed mixes that are a better alternative because they don't contain "all the bad," yet are easy to make.)
➤ boiled eggs
➤ oatmeal
➤ bowl of healthy cereal
➤ fruit smoothies
➤ cheese and crackers
➤ granola bars

➤ **Make healthy snacks easily available.** Create a snack basket that you keep in the pantry with some of your acceptable choices. This makes it easy for you or your children to grab something at the designated time your children are allowed to snack. Having a section in the refrigerator designated for snack items is helpful as well. This creates independence for your older children because they can get what they want on their own and you still know that it is a snack that you approve of.

Planning your menus

Good meals and healthy eating will not happen without good planning. You need to be thoughtful and organized about how you feed your family to ensure that you always have a nutritious meal ready at dinner time. It is not as difficult as you may think once you create a system. In fact, you will impress yourself at how easily you can throw together a great dinner in no time.

➤ **Create a master menu list for your family.** Designate a spot in your day planner for menu ideas for your family. First, make a list of the meals you know that your family loves. Second, make a list of foods that you would like for your family to eat. Hopefully between the two lists, you can come up with at least 14 or so complete meals. Take these two lists and make a master menu list by alternating the meals so you have one meal that you know your family loves and then one that you want them to try. Make sure that the list includes vegetables as well as the entrée.

➤ **When planning your menus, make sure that each meal contains at least one thing you know each of your children like.** It is impossible and poor training to prepare individual meals for each child based on what he does or does not like. Your children should eat, or at least taste, what you have served for supper. If you know there is something on their plate that they like, you know your children will get some of the calories they need even if they refuse to eat all of the other foods you have served. Doing this helps you to stick to your guns about not serving your children something different from the rest of the family because you know they will eat well at least one thing you served.

➤ **Decide how many meals you need to cook a week.** If you always have enough leftovers for a second meal, or if you like to eat out on the weekends, include that into your equation. What you are trying to do is establish how many meals you actually need to cook per week and what days you should plan to cook them. An example of my master meal list for one week looks like the following:

Monday: Crock pot turkey, salad, carrots, corn on the cob, wild rice, and wheat rolls.
Tuesday: Leftovers
Wednesday: Spaghetti, salad, and a wheat baguette.
Thursday: Chicken in mushroom sauce, butterbeans, and wheat wide pasta noodles.
Friday: Leftovers
Saturday: Grilled salmon, salad, asparagus, carrots, and yellow **rice**.
Sunday: Grilled turkey burgers, oven-baked sweet potato fries and coleslaw.

This is a sample of what your weekly menu might look like. Some weeks I only cook a complete meal three or four nights a week depending on how much leftover food we have or what our weekend looks like. You should be able to look at your day planner and know how much you need to cook for the week based on what you have planned.

If you have at least 14 menus lined out, it can carry you for about four weeks because of leftovers and eating out. You can repeat your weekly menus every couple of weeks or add to them as you find new recipes. I always like to try at least one new meal a month in order to broaden my menu selection and keep cooking fun. The master menu list will give you a foundation to feed your family and make meal planning much easier.

➤ **On Sundays, write out your menu for the week and make up a grocery list of what you will need**. Always check to see what you already have in your pantry and refrigerator before you add something to the list; this prevents having duplicates of the same item. Knowing in advance what you are going to prepare every night for the entire week allows you to shop once without having to go to the store more than necessary. It also takes the guesswork out of your day when you are wondering what you are going to feed the family.

Tips for easy meal preparations

➤ **Cut your effort in half by preparing for two meals at once**. You can use your planned weekly menu to help you be more efficient in your food preparation. For instance, if you know you are going to make spaghetti and tacos the same week, you can brown all the meat you need for both meals at one time and refrigerate the amount you need for later. This helps save on prep time and clean up. If you know you will need diced onions for several recipes that week, chop the amount you will need all at once so it will be easier for you later. Thinking ahead can save you a lot of time and energy. You can only do this, however, if you know what you are going to serve for the whole week. This is one of the benefits of weekly menu planning. If you can look at your whole week of meals, you will see where you can save time and plan out you meals to make the most of your time and energy.

➤ **Make the most of your leftovers**. Schedule your weekly meals to allow you to use the leftovers from one meal to help make another. If you are going to grill chicken one night, grill some extra pieces and then use them for quesadillas on another night. Get creative and you will end up saving a lot of time and have easy wonderful meals for your family to enjoy!

➤ **Double the recipe of the food you are making and then freeze half of it for later.** You will have a delicious meal that you can just pull out of the freezer, thaw, and serve. This is a wonderful thing on days when you have to work late or are running around at various activities all afternoon and evening. Properly label and date everything you freeze so you can easily find what you need.

➤ **Use a crock-pot to have a great meal without having to do all the preparation at the last minute.** You can put everything together first thing in the morning or even the night before. If you prepare it the night before, just put the meal together in the pullout dish and place it in the refrigerator. Then, in the morning, set it in the cooker, turn it on low, and you are finished. Crock-pot cooking saved me when we spent all day on the baseball field after school. The family would come home starving, and it was great to walk into the house smelling the aroma of a hot delicious meal. Doing this will also help prevent you from being tempted to grab take-out on a busy day because you know a good meal is at home waiting for you.

➤ **Have your children help prepare for that night's dinner or even the next day's meal.** If your children are of the appropriate age, have them help in any way they can. Children love to open cans, pour things together, stir, chop vegetables, etc. It is also a great help to have vegetables chopped or peeled for the next day's meal in an effort to save time later. This is an excellent way to teach your children how to be useful in the kitchen, give you a helping hand and it is an opportunity for quality time together. And do not forget, this concept also applies to husbands.

➤ **Lay out the nonperishable items for your meal in the morning so you can easily put it together that afternoon or evening.** This also helps you see if you are missing something that you may need to pick up on the way home.

➤ **Do not feel like you have to prepare elaborate side dishes with your meal every night.** Most uncooked vegetables are healthier for you than their cooked counterpart. (Tomatoes are one of those rare exceptions.) If your children prefer uncooked carrots for supper versus cooked ones that are in a fancy sauce, then by all means serve them the uncooked ones. Why add the extra fat, calories and preparation time if your children like them uncooked and the vegetables are healthier served that way? It is great to expose them to different tastes and recipes, but this applies to basic everyday eating. Once I thought this through, I stopped pushing the squash casserole and just let them eat squash. The goal is to help them develop a taste for the vegetables themselves. This can be better accomplished if they are not covered in butter and cheese.

➤ **Utilize kitchen gadgets that can help you work faster in the kitchen.** A heavy duty mixer that can be working while you are doing something else for a recipe is worth its weight in gold. A food processor that grates cheese in seconds saves a lot of time as compared to a hand grater. (I always grate my own cheese because the pre-grated just does not taste as good.) An onion slicer is also a great tool to help speed things along. Think about what you do most in the kitchen and decide what tools could help you do it more quickly.

➤ **If you have the opportunity, switch over to a gas stove.**

The speed at which it heats up and cooks food is amazing and can be a great time saver.

➤ **Store items that you use for a specific task together in the same location.** For example, your cutting boards should be kept near your kitchen knives. You should not have to walk all over your kitchen opening drawers here and there for items that are always used together.

➤ **At the end of the week, look in your refrigerator and pantry and create a meal that uses the items you already have so no go to waste.** This is great if you did not have the leftovers that you anticipated and need an extra meal at the end of the week. When this happens to me, I love to use the extra vegetables I have to make a big pot of spaghetti. That extra bell pepper, onion, and leftover mushrooms are well utilized in a dish like this. Not only do you have a savory dish, but you will not have to throw out any vegetables that have not been used in previous meals. Stir-fry is another great meal that can make use of extra vegetables or even cooked meats.

➤ **Clean up as you go!** Do not wait until the end of the prep work to start cleaning. You can even have one of your children help clean up as you are cooking. If one child likes to scrub pots, then set him up at the sink and he can go to town. Your kitchen will stay in better order and the task will not be as overwhelming if you put things back after using them and put dirty dishes in the dishwasher as you go.

➤ **Utilize a "trash bowl."** Place one of you large bowls on the counter to throw away scraps as you cook so you are not constantly running back and forth to the garbage can. This saves more time than you might think. Another option is to pull your main garbage can to the area where you are working. Just do not let it hinder your ability to move about the kitchen.

➤ **Try to make sure that your dishwasher is empty before you start preparing dinner.** This allows you to load it as you go and prevents a sink full of dirty dishes.

➤ **Have a "cooking party."** Get together with some friends once a month and put together 10 or so meals that can be frozen and used later. Each person can be in charge of several meals and bring the ingredients she will need to prepare it. Each person can make triple or quadruple the recipe to share with the others. This is a great way to get a lot of cooking accomplished and try out new meals while visiting with friends.

Dinner rituals and table manners

There is something special about a family sitting down to enjoy a meal together. It is an important and special part of family life. Studies continue to prove the importance of this family time and encourage people to make it a priority in their house. If you cannot eat together every night, try to have at least several dinners a week as a family. Your family will benefit from this time to communicate and reconnect with each other.

Dinner rituals

Establishing some family dinner rituals can be a special part of your meals together. Your family may like to take turns sharing something special that happened to them that day or perhaps holding hands to say a prayer before supper. You may even have some dinner rituals from your childhood that you want to continue with your own family. If you have not already established some dinner rituals of your own, give some thought as to what you could do to add to your family's time together at the table.

One of the rituals that our family has, and it is a favorite of mine, is that after we have eaten supper I leave the kitchen to have some time to myself while my husband and four boys put on some good music and clean everything up. It is a nice time for me, and the boys have come to enjoy this time working together with their father. Some other examples of dinner rituals are listed below. Find an idea or two that might work for your family or get creative and create your own.

➤ **Have a "question of the day."** Having great dinner conversation is important to making a meal special. Just the simple, "How was your day?" is not always going to get a lot of conversation going, especially for older children. Get creative and ask open-ended questions. You can make a list of questions that you and your family create and then take turns each night pulling one out of a hat to be discussed at that meal. Some dinner questions could include:

➤ What really made you laugh today?
➤ What is something new that you learned today that really stuck with you or surprised you?
➤ On our next vacation, what kind of trip would you enjoy?
➤ If you won $1,000,000, how would you spend it, and to what charity would you donate some of it?

➤ If you could be anything when you grow up, what would it be and why?

➤ If you could be any animal what would it be and why?

➤ If you could have any question answered, what would it be?

➤ If you could have your favorite meal, what would it be?

➤ If you could invent something, what would it be and why?

➤ If you could live anywhere in the world, where would it be and why?

➤ If you could live during any time period, when would it be and why?

➤ **Choose a "word of the day."** Pick a certain word each night that you would like to add to your children's vocabulary. You may need two words if the ages of your children vary greatly so each has a word appropriate to his age. Give the definition of the word and see if your children can incorporate the word into the conversation during supper. Make it a game and count how many times each person, including adults, can use the word properly.

➤ **Discuss a current event.** You can adapt this ritual to be appropriate for the ages of your children. Discussing world issues is better for older children, since many current events are of a mature nature. However, if you have younger children who are interested in topics such as sports, cooking, or fashion, you could pull out those sections of the paper to have them choose an article to discuss. You can go around the table and ask each person to talk about what he learned from the article he read.

Table manners

Table manners are an important part of the overall dining experience. Dining together is not only an eating experience, but a social one as well. Only when your children are taught how to behave at the table can your family, as well as others with whom you may dine, truly enjoy the meal as it was meant to be.

Good table manners need to be established as early as when your child is in the high chair. Even young children can be taught what is and is not acceptable behavior. For example, throwing food is not acceptable behavior at any age and should never be tolerated. This may be the only form of table manners a baby may have, but it is the beginning of understanding that there are standards to follow.

As your children age, you can add to the list of things that you expect from them at the table. You will have a foundation of manners that you can continue to add to. This is a much easier approach than waiting until your children reach a certain age before you start teaching them good table manners.

Sitting down to eat as a family is important to reinforce and model good table etiquette. If you are running in and out of the kitchen while your children eat or are talking on the phone, it will be harder to teach them good table manners. You also will not be able to follow up on what you expect of your children if you are not in the kitchen with them. This is especially true if your family is in the car and eating on the run. It is important to use the time your family sits down together at the table as an opportunity to teach appropriate behavior and to enforce the rules you have made for your children. If your children know that you will follow up on the rules, they will quickly learn to follow them more closely.

When one of our children acts out of line at the table after being previously corrected, he is sent up to his room for a specified amount of time before he is asked to rejoin the family. This is effective for negative behavior in our house because everyone loves dinner time. If they have misbehaved, we also do not let them eat dessert (if it is being served), even if they ate everything on their plate.

You could also set up a reward system for your children to reinforce their good behavior. Maybe they could earn a sticker for a chart you create, earn an extra bedtime story, or be exempt from cleaning up after supper.

Having table manners established allows for your family to enjoy one of the most important parts of a family meal—the social interaction. This is the time to talk with the whole family and update everyone on the day's or week's events and just visit as a family. You are also teaching your children how to interact in a group setting and how to carry on a good conversation with each other. The conversation at the table should allow ample time for each person to talk about what he chooses, as long as it is appropriate, of course. Maintaining a strict rule about not interrupting each other is very important to make each child feel like what he is saying is valuable and to show respect for the person talking. Children should also be expected to listen to the adult conversation and not allowed to monopolize everything that is discussed at the table.

Provide a positive atmosphere at the dinner table, and as your children age they will see this family time as an important part of their lives and make a stronger effort to be there. When they hit adolescence and go through the struggles that face teens, this time together can be a tremendous comfort for them as well as a way to help everyone to stay connected.

6

Shopping Simplified

SOME PEOPLE LOVE TO SHOP AND FIND GREAT PLEASURE IN IT. There are also others that see it as an unavoidable necessity of life and do it only because they have to. No matter in which of these two groups you fall, simplifying shopping is important. Now that you have children, your time and money are becoming more and more valuable, and learning how to save on both should be a priority.

We all know that as your family increases in size, so do your shopping needs. You go through more and more food and clothing as your children grow as well as with each additional child you add to your brood. You need to become a master at shopping in an effort to save you precious time and money. Being organized is the first step to take you in this direction.

If you have already implemented some of the previous systems in this book, you are off to a head start by being more organized. An organized pantry, for example, allows you to quickly see what you already have and what you may need to purchase. An organized closet allows you to keep better track of what you own, which prevents you from buying a garment that is a duplicate of something you already have. Have menus planned out for the week enables you to go to the grocery store only once a week instead of every few days. As you can see, becoming a better shopper is yet another benefit of having your home and life organized.

Grocery shopping made easy

Most Americans make more trips to the grocery store than necessary. Planning your meals out for the week is important to help prevent those extra trips that zap your time and energy. You should only have to go to the grocery store once a week if you know what you will be eating every day. Follow the following simple steps to help make your grocery shopping more efficient and less stressful:

➤ **Create a master grocery shopping list.** It is very helpful to write or print out a standard grocery list for you to make copies of and use again and again. We all shop for basically the same items week after week, and if you have a standard grocery list you can simply highlight each item as you need it. Listing the items by category or aisle really helps to speed up the shopping process. You can organize your list by fruits and vegetables, dairy, meats, products such as aluminum foil, or toilet paper, etc. If you repeatedly shop at the same store, you may choose to make your list according to how that store is organized. This reduces the time you spend in the store going back and forth from aisle to aisle. You can even ask if the store has a layout of the way it is organized to help you create your list. (I did this once when I moved to a new town, and it was a huge help in finding my way around the store and shopping more efficiently.)

Let everyone in the family know where the list is so they can highlight or add something to it as is needed. Do not forget to leave space to add items that you need to purchase that are not already listed.

➤ **Make your weekly grocery list.** Once you have written down which meals you will serve for the week, make your grocery list for the items you will need. Always check your pantry and refrigerator first to see if you already own some of the ingredients. After you have made your list, add to it the other items you will need to get through the week.

➤ **Shop for deals.** If you are looking to save some money and have close access to several stores, you may want to scan the paper for store specials. This can save you a lot of money on the larger ticket items such as meat. Buying in bulk and freezing extra is a smart way to save on your food bill. It would be helpful to even find the deals before you plan your weekly menu so you can use what is on sale. I like to scan the Sunday paper to see what is a good deal and then plan my weekly menu accordingly.

If your stores are out of the way, it may not be worth the extra gas and effort to do this, but if you do have stores close by, it is well worth your time. Even if you shop at the same store week after week, you can use their store specials to help plan your menu.

Getting to know what the costs of items you buy repeatedly is important to help save money. You will quickly know when there is a great deal on products when you are aware of their normal costs. I love the "buy one get one free" items if they are something I normally purchase. If you have the extra pantry space, take advantage of these sales. Do not, however, fall into the trap of buying something just because it is on sale. Who cares how much you save if it is something you did not want in the first place?

➤ **To coupon or not to coupon?** You have to decide if clipping coupons is worth your time and energy. If items that you regularly purchase have good coupons available, then it may pay off for you to go through them. Remember, do not clip coupons for items that you would not have purchased just because you can save money on that particular product. If you do like to redeem coupons, purchase a small binder to keep them organized so you can easily find the coupon that you need. Go through the binder periodically to purge the ones that have expired.

➤ **Shopping with the kids**. If you take your children to the grocery store with you, you know that it can either go really well or really bad. Start your children off with good shopping habits to help make your life easier and to prevent yourself from buying all the extras that they ask for.

➤ *If you never buy your children a candy bar at the checkout, they will never ask for one.* My children knew it just was not an option and it would amaze friends when we would go shopping when they did not ask for anything. If I ever did purchase something impulsive, such as gum, I made it clear that this was an exception and not to expect it the next time. This prevents your children from getting into the "can I have it?" syndrome at the check-out.

➤ *Beware of the free cookie!* If you feel you must get the free cookie that many stores offer for children, do what you need to do. I did not find it to be healthy or good training. If you think your child is going to get hungry while you shop, bring a healthy snack with you or purchase one for him to eat. You do not want your children to get into the "I must have a cookie to make it through the store" mentality or have them munching on a cookie at eight in the morning.

➤ *Shop fast!* If you have your list organized and can shop quickly, your children should be able to make it through the experience with ease. You do have to work it, though. Talk to your children and ask for help looking for items. Let them put vegetables in the bag or unload the items onto the checkout counter. If they are part of the experience, they will enjoy shopping more and behave better.

➤ *You may find it helpful to bring toys in with your children to play with while riding in the cart.* I tried this and only found myself picking them up over and over again. For me, it took more time than it was worth. I was also paranoid that one of my children would accidentally launch one of the toys at a passing shopper—not because they were aggressive, just highly athletic and loved to show off their skills. If you, however, find that bringing in some toys helps to keep your children occupied, you could use a small canvas tote bag as a "Shopping Bag" and put a couple of small toys and a few books in it. Every time you make a trip to the store with your children, you could bring the tote for them to play with. Keep it special by only allowing the toys to be used while shopping.

➤ *Be prepared to leave the store with your children if they cannot behave properly.* Some children learn quickly that they can get away with things in a store that they normally cannot. If you make it clear that you will load back up in the car and leave if your children do not behave as they should, and then actually do it when necessary, behavior will improve. If you have to leave a full shopping cart in a store because one of your children is misbehaving, it will be an inconvenience but well worth it down the road. Your children will remember it the next time, and their behavior should improve. (As a side note, I have also done this while eating in a restaurant. If someone misbehaved repeatedly, my husband or I would take him out to the car and sit with him for a while before we returned to our table. Consequently, we are now able to enjoy eating out with all six of us, and it is a pleasurable experience.)

Shopping for your family and home

➤ **As you discover you need to purchase non-grocery items for your family or your home, write them down in a designated place in your planner.** If it is something that you do not need immediately, you can keep your list together until you have the opportunity to go shopping. This keeps what you need organized so that nothing is forgotten, and it helps you consolidate your shopping trips so you do not head to the stores every time you need to make a purchase. You also may discover that something you thought you needed or wanted is not really necessary. If you let some time pass, an item that you wanted at first may no longer seem important. Become a better shopper by using the time between recognizing a need and purchasing it to find a good deal or to do research on the product you want. By being thoughtful in what you buy, you will be happier with your purchase and will receive a better value for your money.

It is also very helpful to anticipate your purchasing needs before something becomes an emergency, forcing you to immediately run out to buy it.

Try to stay out of the stores as much as possible. This will ultimately save you time from numerous shopping trips and money because you will not be tempted to purchase items that you do not need. If you are running to the stores several times a week, you need to reevaluate your shopping habits. Decide which days you will designate to shopping and stick to it. This can help prevent impulsive shopping trips. The less you are in the stores, the less you will spend and the more time you will have.

7

Keeping Your Family Healthy and Active

TODAY'S WORLD HAS BECOME MUCH MORE SEDENTARY THAN in the past. Neighborhoods that used to be filled with children playing are now mostly empty because many of the kids are in the house on the computer, playing video games, or watching television. This fact has had a very negative effect on the weight and overall health of our younger generation. It is up to us as parents to help provide an atmosphere for our children that promotes good health and physical activity.

Television and video games

Parents have the responsibility to help ensure that their children are staying active. I have heard parents complain that their children do not like to play outside and just want to watch television or play video games. When I have suggested they get rid of those items that cause them so much grief, they look at me in horror. In my mind, if something is preventing your child from staying active and healthy, it should be strictly regulated if not gotten rid of all together.

You would never allow your children to eat ice cream for every meal each day of the week, even though your children would probably love it. You would not allow this because you know it would not be healthy for them. Children need you to restrict how much media time they get in order to stay healthy, just as they need you to regulate how much ice cream they eat.

You are the parent and can determine how much media your child views or participates in. With all of the stimulating shows and games that are available for children now, they need and expect you to help set limits.

➤ **Set rules for how much TV, computer, or video game time you children are allowed.** Studies show that this is extremely important and that most children are logging in way too much time on these activities. When your child is not participating in media time, he will be doing other things that can be enriching and improve social skills. We have been programmed to believe that all of the excessive time children, as well as adults, spend in front of a TV or video game is just a part of modern day life; however, it does not have to be that way.

If your children have been allowed unlimited access to the television, videos, or the computer, it is time to decide what a good time limit is for each and enforce your new rules.

➤ **Life can exist without television.** I know some of you may find it hard to believe, but it is true. My husband and I got rid of our television after being married just under two years. We decided that it was not good use of our time because after working all day and being apart, we wanted to visit with each other and not sit around staring at a TV watching other people lead their lives. It was one of the best decisions we have ever made. Our quality of life and our relationship improved just by selling the TV set, and we never watched much of it from the start.

We went about 13 years without owning a television and loved it. Our children grew up not knowing who Barney was, and it did not seem to bother them in the least bit. They were not set in front of the electronic babysitter so that I could cook supper or just have some quiet time. They played instead. They played a lot and read a lot. They did things that they would not have otherwise done if they had been watching TV.

Our children also did not ask for all of the junk that is advertised during cartoons. For Christmas they would ask for a football or baseball cards and not the items being advertised to other children. They did not beg to have the high-sugared cereals that are pushed on Saturday mornings. They were not being commercialized to death.

We did finally purchase a television to watch our college alma mater play baseball in the World Series; we are big sport fans. We made it very clear to the children, then ages 8, 6, 5, and 2½, that this was a TV that would be used only occasionally and was not going to become a part of our normal life. We have stuck to that rule and only have it on for major sporting events and for a family movie maybe twice a month. Because our children are not used to having access to television at all, they do not ask to watch it and do not expect it. The rare occasion when they are allowed to watch a movie is seen as a treat, and they enjoy it.

Help your children by making the decision to find what is in good balance for your family and stick to it.

Getting more exercise

If you have placed strict guidelines for television and video games, it will make increasing exercise easier. Because of our lack of TV viewing, our children are constantly outside playing and running around. In fact, it is hard to get them to come inside because they enjoy it so much. If you have a big yard or a neighborhood that is conducive for pick-up games or bike riding, etc., keeping your children physically active should be easy. If you do not, you have to get more creative and be more intentional to help your children get the exercise they need. Try some of these suggestions to help your children get active. In the process you may find yourself becoming a little more active too.

➤ Ride bikes together
➤ Go for a walk
➤ Play tag
➤ Throw the ball
➤ Jump rope together
➤ Play a pick-up game with some neighbors
➤ Buy a basketball hoop to shoot baskets
➤ Create an exercise routine that you can do together.
➤ Measure out a certain distance and time how fast your children can run it. Run the same distance several times a week and see how much they can improve their time and keep a record of it. Even little ones can do this for a short distance, and don't forget to record Mom and Dad's time too!
➤ Do push-up and sit-ups together

➤ Hit a tennis ball back and forth
➤ Go to a park and play
➤ Take a weekend hike
➤ Go for a long walk at the beach
➤ Visit your county park and walk or ride the trails

As you can see, there are limitless ways to log in some extra exercise. The goal is to make sure your family is being physically active and have it become a part of their life. What activity level your children are raised in now will determine what they do later. Children that are brought up exercising typically end up leading active lives as adults. This fact results in a decrease in the odds that they become overweight or obese and can reduce their risks for health problems. Remember, children are meant to run and be active. It is your job to ensure that they do!

Fast food and junk food

What you and your family eat has a great impact on your overall health. Refer to Chapter 5, "How to Feed Your Family", where healthy food choices and good eating habits are discussed.

8

Entertaining, Birthday Parties and Holidays

IF YOU ARE LIKE ME, OPENING YOUR HOME TO SHARE WITH others is something you take great pleasure in. Throwing a party and having friends and family get-together is a wonderful and important part of life. Unfortunately, once people have children, the amount of entertaining they do can lessen due to the extra effort it takes. Now that you have your home organized and an established cleaning system in place, this does not need to be the case. If you are organized and thoughtful in your planning, entertaining will be a pleasurable experience for you and your family as well as the guest you entertain.

If you are implementing the principles in this book, you will find that entertaining in your home will already be less stressful because your house is kept in good order. Having the basic housekeeping standards established in your home will allow you to focus on the entertaining aspect of a get together and not the cleaning part. That is step one.

Step two is to have an organized game plan of what you need to do and a schedule of when you are to do it. This is true whether you are having a formal sit-down dinner, a child's birthday party, or are throwing a large adult party for 50 people. Having a good game plan will take the stress out of your preparations and ensure you do not forget something at the last minute.

Stress-free guide to planning a party

Once you have decided to have a get-together, sit down with your day planner and start getting organized. Follow the tips below to help take the stress out of preparing for you party and to ensure your party is a success.

➤ **Pick a date and time for your get-together, including what time it should start and end.**

➤ **Decide if it is to be an adult only or kid-friendly party.** (For a child's birthday party, see the tips in the next section.)

➤ **Determine what kind of party you are having.** Is it going to be a luncheon, formal sit-down dinner, cocktail party, or a backyard barbecue?

➤ **Pick a theme for the party.** This will affect what invitations and decorations you will use as well as the type of food that you will serve. This may be dictated by the time of year your party is given. If it is a small gathering, this may simply refer to the choice of colors you use for flowers and napkins.

➤ **Make your guest list.** For a large party it is helpful to make an "A" list for those people you know you definitely want to attend and a "B" list for those people you would like to attend if you can afford the additional cost and the space in your home.

➤ **Create the menu.** Pull out all of your favorite recipes and decide what coordinates with your party. Use recipes that you know. A party is not a good time to experiment with something new. If you would like to use a dish or appetizer you have never made before, try it out ahead of time so you will know if you like it and exactly how to prepare it. Always make sure that you have a balance between what can only be done at the last minute and what you can prepare ahead to balance your workload.

➤ **Let your guests help out.** If you are having a casual get-together with close friends, decide what you will prepare and have a list of options for your guest if you are going to request that they bring something. If I do this for a meal, I like to provide the main and side dishes and then ask others to bring an appetizer, salad, or dessert. When you prepare the core menu, you do not have to worry if a side dish someone brings will complement the entrée you are preparing because you still have control of the main meal. This also allows your guests to share something they really want to prepare while taking some of the work load off of you. For a get-together with familiar friends, I have found that people are usually happy to contribute and usually ask what they can bring.

➤ **If you are going to have the party catered, start contacting respected caterers in your area for ideas and costs.** You can have the caterer do everything, or you may decide to have some of the food catered and some that you prepare yourself to mix it up and to cut down the cost.

➤ **Create a section in your planner designated for everything relating to your party for easy reference.**

➤ **Make a master list of what you need to do to prepare for your party in your day planner.** Organize your master list into four categories according to when each task should be completed. Now that you know what type of party you are having, about how many people to expect, and what foods will be served, you can create you master schedule of everything there is to do.

Organize your list into the following four categories: (1) weeks before the party, (2) week of the party, (3) two days before the party, and (4) day of the party. The example written out below gives you a guide from which to create your own master party list. How you organize your party planning will vary depending on what type of get-together you are having.

1. Weeks before the party

➤ Prepare invitations. This should be the first on your list so that you can get them picked out, printed, and mailed at least two-and-a-half weeks before the party. If you are having a small, casual get-together and will simply call your friends, decide what day you will contact them. Be sure to call them early enough to allow time for them to plan; this also increases the odds that they will be available to attend.

➤ Locate and wash platters or hors d'oeuvre trays that you

will be using to see if you need to purchase or borrow anything.

➤ Polish silver.

➤ Choose decorations and centerpieces.

➤ Address any small home project you may want to have completed before the party.

➤ Prepare any foods ahead of time that you are able to freeze for the party.

➤ Book a caterer, if using one.

➤ Line up a babysitter if it is an adult-only party.

➤ Wash and iron any linens you may be using.

➤ Choose the music you want to be played during the party. You can even create a customized playlist of music according to what your theme is or who your guests will be.

➤ Pick out your party clothes. Decide what you and your family will wear. This will allow enough time for you to have something dry cleaned or the time to shop for something new.

2. Week of the party

➤ Make your grocery list for everything you will need. Separate the items you can purchase ahead of time from the ones you need to get a day before the party.

➤ Shop early in the week for non-perishable foods and beverages.

➤ Order flowers.

➤ Lay out the trays or dishes you will be using with a sticky note labeling what food will go in which dish.

➤ Give the house a deep clean or have a cleaning service help out.

➤ Wipe down your outdoor furniture.

➤ Mow and weed the yard.

➤ Try to enlist a close friend or family member to come to the party a little early to help out with the last-minute things that need attending to. (This is usually only necessary for large parties.)

3. Two days before the party

➤ Shop for the remaining items on your grocery list.

➤ Prepare any dishes that can be put together this far in advance. It is helpful even if you are only able to prepare part of the dish ahead of time. For example, dice vegetables, mix a sauce together that will be used in a recipe, prepare a marinade, etc.

➤ Set your table. If you are having a sit-down supper, you can go ahead and set your table. If it is a cocktail party with hors d'oeuvres, lay your trays out exactly how you want them presented on your table. This includes linens, any risers you may use to add height to your table, or decorative pieces, etc. This helps you to not only prepare ahead, but allows you to see if you are missing anything or need to add something to the table. If you have small children in the house, use caution in what you set out so that no one gets hurt and nothing is broken.

➤ Write out the time table for everything that will occur the day of the party. This should include things such as when to put the ice out, when to preheat the oven and to what temperature, when and what foods need to be put in and taken out of the oven, etc. Keep your schedule out indiscreetly or put it in your pocket so that you can easily refer to it throughout the party. It is much easier to refer to a schedule versus having to work it through in your mind while you are trying to serve as a hostess. If you are having a sit-down dinner, list all of the items on the menu so you make sure not to forget something. This step is key to being a graceful and stress-free entertainer!

4. Day of the party

➤ Put together the food items that must be prepared at the last minute.

➤ Put flowers out.

➤ Sweep porches and walks.

➤ Final quick clean of the house. Pay close attention to the guest bathroom. People have a lot of time to just sit and stare while they are using the restroom. Your guest bathroom should be immaculate at the beginning of the party and then it is always a good idea to check it throughout the party. Not every person is as neat as you may want them to be, especially if there are children attending, and a once-over in the bathroom may be needed several times during the party. I like to keep disposable cleaning wipes under the sink so that I can tidy up unnoticed.

➤ Turn on the music.

➤ Adjust the lighting to the way you want it.

➤ Fill the ice bucket or cooler with plenty of ice.

➤ Have several trash cans accessible.

➤ Get yourself ready. Allow plenty of time to get yourself ready. Try to be ready at least an hour before the party is to begin. You want to be ready in case you have unexpected early arrivals. My thought is that early guests can help you fill the ice bucket, but they are not going to help you apply makeup to your face. This also keeps you both from being in an awkward situation if you have to excuse yourself to finish getting ready. Get ready a little early and then worry about the rest of your to-do list. Also, make sure your spouse is ready early too so he can help out with the last-minute things instead of being in the shower while you are running around.

➤ Make sure your dishwasher is empty to help keep the kitchen tidy during the party.

Write out which task should be completed on which days on your planner's daily sheets. Now that you have your master list, you can plan out exactly when to do each thing. This will help you stay on track.

If you follow your schedule, it should keep you from feeling overwhelmed before the party so you can enjoy it as much as your guests. You will reap the rewards of being organized by having a successful party without taxing you or your family. You will also find that the more you entertain, the easier it gets.

How to throw a successful birthday party

For your child's birthday party or any other child-themed party, the concepts listed above still apply, but you also have to take into account the attention span and needed activities for the age group in attendance. For young children, a party that is an hour-and-a-half to two hours long is ample time to get together. Saturday parties are often common, but consider a Friday afternoon party so it does not conflict with family time. With so many demands on families these days, it is easy to pass on a birthday party that falls on a Saturday or Sunday. Help increase attendance and be sensitive to the families you want to attend by scheduling your party on a Friday afternoon or even a day during the week.

➤ **Make a schedule for the party's activities.** Once you establish the date and time of your party, list out the activities you plan to have and the time each one will take. Try to have several activities for the children, but do not overdo it. Write out a schedule in your planner that states each activity along with the time you want to allow for it until the ending time of the party. An example follows:

> 3:00–3:30 — Guests arrive, work on crafts and have snacks
> 3:30–4:00 — Scavenger Hunt
> 4:00–4:15 — Sing Happy Birthday and eat cake
> 4:15–4:30 — Open presents
> 4:30–4:45 — Piñata
> 5:00 — Guests leave

Before the party, make a copy of the schedule to keep in your pocket so you can refer to it easily. When you have the layout for your party lined up, there is no guesswork and guests know that they will be able to leave at the time they anticipated. I have been to many a party that was scheduled to end after two hours to find that after that time we had not even sung "Happy Birthday." Respect your guests by sticking to your schedule. Everyone is very busy, and they have made the effort to attend your child's party. Appreciate their effort by not holding them hostage at your party. Typically people feel bad if they have to leave before you sing "Happy Birthday" so avoid putting your guests in that situation by staying on schedule.

➤ **Opening presents.** If your child is going to open up presents at the party, give him a pep talk before the party begins. Make sure that he knows that he is to read the card first and look the guest in the eye and thank him after he has opened the gift. Prepare him as well for a duplicate gift and instruct him on how to handle it so that he does not hurt the feeling of the giver. If your child is not old enough to do this, then it is your job to receive the gifts well. Some people are avoiding the ritual of having their children open up presents at the party. I feel that it helps them to learn how to receive gifts properly and is an exciting part of the party for children.

➤ **Thank you notes.** Make sure that if your child opens up presents when the guests are there that someone writes down who gave him what. This is very helpful when writing thank you notes. If your child is old enough to write, have him complete the thank you notes himself. If he is too young, you can write them out and have your child write his name or draw a picture on it to personalize the note. It is good to teach your children that thank you notes are a must. Try to involve them in the process as early as possible. Pace yourself and try to do a couple per night if it is too much for your child to write them all out in one sitting. Set a goal to get them out within the first week of the party. The longer you wait, the harder it is to get them completed.

Holidays without the hassle

Holidays can be the best time of the year for your family, but it can also be a stressful one if you are not careful. One thing that helps you to stay organized for a holiday is that you know exactly when it will be year after year. This piece of knowledge can help you plan better for the events and activities that accompany each holiday. There are some things that you can do well in advance to help alleviate some of the pressure as the holiday approaches.

Look at Christmas, for example. If you send out cards to all of your friends and family members every year, then this is an opportunity to work ahead. You can address the envelopes in October or November, so that is one less thing you have to do in December. Understand that by doing things ahead of time you are not taking away from the enjoyment of the holiday, but you are actually allowing yourself to enjoy it more and enjoy each particular to its fullest.

I always have a great time holiday shopping for people throughout the year because I am able to put more focus on that one person and be more thoughtful in the gift I buy. It is a much better experience than having to buy gifts for all of your friends and family members in a one-time shopping spree. If you do it at the last minute, you will not only have the stress of needing to get it all done, but you may not find that perfect gift, and you will usually end up spending more money.

Listed below are some points that can make your holidays go more smoothly and allow you and your family to enjoy this special time even more:

➤ **Keep a gift list.** List in your day planner the people for whom you know you will be buying gifts, whether it is for a birthday or for a holiday such as Christmas. Next, make a column for gift ideas and another for gifts you have actually purchased for that person. As you think of ideas for someone or hear him mention something that he wants or needs, jot it down on this page. This will allow you to purchase that item from a catalog, while out shopping, or better yet, when it is on sale. Then note on your "gift page" what you purchased and how much it costs. Documenting how much you spend allows you to stay within a budget and helps to balance out your children's gifts so you spend about the same amount on each. It also helps if you set a goal for when you want all of your shopping completed. My goal is to have Christmas shopping completed before Thanksgiving.

➤ **Pick out and address your holiday cards early.** Having your cards ready to be mailed early is an easy way to stay ahead. I used to do all of my cards while we were on long road trips. (A lapboard is great to use in the car to help do things such as this.) If you purchase cards after the holiday is over, you can get a great deal on them and you have them to address early for the next year. You will enjoy writing out your cards more because you will be able to give each one extra attention and have the time to write in personal notes.

➤ **Plan out your menus early.** Whether you are throwing a holiday party or having the family over for a big meal, early planning makes it easier. Refer to the section earlier in this chapter about how to plan a party.

➤ **Make cookies and candies early.** Most young children are interested in the decorating part of holiday cookies and do not have the attention span to go through the entire process. It is helpful to make ahead and freeze cookie dough for cut-out or sugar cookies that can be decorated later. You can even take it one step further and go ahead and actually make the cookies to freeze. Certain candy recipes also freeze well and are great to keep on hand. If unexpected guests arrive, you will always have a special treat to offer and you can prepare ahead for future get-togethers. Candies also make for great little gifts that you can prepare ahead.

➤ **Decorate early and in phases**. It is fun to get your house ready for a holiday, and by doing it early, you can enjoy the decorations longer. Working a little early will also prevent you from doing it when you know you have other holiday-related tasks to complete. If you decorate in two or more phases, it will not be as overwhelming. For example, if you celebrate Christmas, you can put out the indoor decorations first, then put up the lights outside (even if you do not turn them on yet), and lastly put up a tree and decorate it. Set your goal for completion and then do the same thing when it is time to take all of the decorations down. Note in you day planner if there is anything that you need to purchase for that year or for the next year that you could purchase during the post-holiday sales.

➤ **Line out party clothes early**. Whenever you get an invitation or know that you are going to throw a party, start thinking about what you and your family will wear. This will allow you to shop early for that perfect outfit or to take clothes to the cleaners.

➤ **Keep a record of gifts received**. Record who gives your family what gift in your planner to refer to later when you are writing your thank you notes.

➤ **Relax and enjoy!** Once you have children, if not before, things do not always go as planned. Be prepared for such things by keeping a good attitude and understanding this reality in life. Find humor in a situation instead of letting it frustrate you to help keep things upbeat. What may seem like a disaster today will be great for telling stories and getting a laugh years down the road.

9

Taking Care of You

THIS IS NOT THE LAST CHAPTER BECAUSE IT IS THE LEAST important; actually, it is one of the most important. Moms hear how important it is to take care of themselves all the time, but rarely do they take the advice to heart. Having time for yourself is extremely important and will ultimately make you a better parent and person. You are required to give so much of yourself 24 hours/seven days a week, and you need to have time to recharge.

Making time for yourself can mean many things. Yes, it means getting a massage or having a girls' weekend, but it also means taking the few minutes at home to paint your nails, soak in a tub, or read a good book. After reading this chapter you should find it possible to make time for yourself by acknowledging its importance and realizing it is easier than you may have previously thought.

Decide what you want to do and how to do It

➤ **What do you really want to do?** Decide what is important to you that is outside the realm of your family. Do you like to play tennis, work out, spend time with your girlfriends, or volunteer, or do you have any other special interest that you have neglected? Write down in the goal section of your day planner what interests you want to pursue and start figuring out how you can do it. You will feel more like a complete person and not just a mom if you are able to do even just one thing that is important to you. Realize that being a mom is the most important thing you could be, and I am not trying to take away from that. I am suggesting, however, that you can be a better mom if you do something for yourself that interests you and makes you happy. List what you want to do in the order of importance and decide what fits into your life at this time.

➤ **How to find the time.** Ask your spouse or other family members for their support in accomplishing what you want. Be realistic in your goals but also try to make it happen. If you have been dying to get back into tennis, wanting to play four days a week is probably not realistic, especially if you work full-time and have young children. However, two days a week might be possible. Let your family know how important it is to you and recruit their help and support.

You will not always be able to utilize the help of others and need to rely on your own creativity to find some time for yourself. With the demands of four young children, I had to learn to get creative with my time in order to feel like I was taking care of myself.

Working out in a gym and running has always been a part of my life, but it was getting pushed aside due to my husband's work demands and the ages of my children. I decided that staying healthy and being in shape was worth getting up at 5:30 a.m. to go to the gym to get my exercise in. I would work out while the rest of my family slept, and then I was back at home in time to prepare breakfast and get everyone out the door on time for school. Once I started doing this I felt so much better about myself and had more energy, even though I was getting up earlier. I had to create the time I needed to do what I wanted and it worked.

Think how you can get creative in an effort to steal time to do what you want to do. I had to apply this principle in writing this book. I always joked that no one had written a book with young children addressing the issues I have discussed because all of us moms were in the weeds and could never find the time to do it. I knew that if I wanted to take on the task, I had to really search for the time to write. I worked on this book on my laptop in car line, when my youngest napped, after they went to bed and any other moment I could steal. Time will not fall into your lap for you to do what you want. You have to make it happen, or it won't!

Simple ways to find a babysitter

If you do not have family that live close by or is able to help you out, find a good babysitter that you can trust. Even if you do have family members who can baby-sit, it is still good to have a sitter or two who can watch your children when needed. Listed are some of the many ways to search for a sitter:

➤ **Referrals**. Asking other parents if they can refer someone to you is the best approach because you can get someone with a proven track record.

➤ **Local colleges or universities**. Call the school's career center and find out how to post a job description. Be detailed in what you are looking for. If you have a regular schedule for which you need help, include the days and times you need.

➤ **Professional caregivers at your gym**. A lot of times caregivers at your gym are happy to pick up some extra cash babysitting. If you like how a person interacts with your child and appears to be responsible, ask her if she is available to sit for you. This is a good method to find help because you get a sneak preview of who she is and how well she plays with your child. Ask at your gym if they perform background checks on their caregivers. This can be another advantage of using their caregivers as well.

➤ **Caregivers at your church, temple, or synagogue**. The same benefits apply here as stated above.

➤ **Online nanny services**. There are many websites that can help match you up with a professional caregiver. This is really helpful for someone who is looking for a full-time nanny or one that will work a lot of regular hours.

➤ **Family friends**. Ask other parents of older children if their child baby-sits. Knowing a family is comforting, and the sitter may already have a relationship with you and your child.

➤ **Centers that teach babysitting courses**. Your local Red

Cross or community hospital may offer such courses and are a great way to find someone who is going to taking babysitting seriously. They usually train the students in first aid and infant/child CPR as well as teaching them how to be effective sitters.

➤ **Swap babysitting with a friend.** This can be a great method if you are on a tight budget. Ask your friends if they are interested in watching your children one day or night if you return the favor for them. If your children are similar in age, it can be a fun time for them and allows you to get to know your friend's children better.

➤ **Post an ad in a local newspaper.** This is my least favorite method because you have no idea whom you are going to get. If you choose to use this approach, make sure you have an organized format for a phone interview to help weed through the applicants.

Interviewing applicants

If someone contacts you from an ad, be it from the college's career center or from the newspaper, try to cover as much ground as you can on the phone prior to setting up an interview. You do not want to waste your time or hers if you can easily determine during a phone interview that she may not be who you are looking for. Discuss her experience, availability, and expected pay, and just try to get an overall feel for who she is. If you decide to set up an interview, ask her to bring references from families she has sat with before. Making the effort to call families she has worked with is very helpful when deciding whether you want to hire her or not.

When you do meet with a candidate, have your children with you to see how they take to her. Allow for some time to get to know the person. Remember, you are looking for someone who not only interacts well with your children, but who is responsible and can handle an emergency. You also need someone who will be dependable.

Having someone who is trained in infant and child CPR is something to strongly consider. Babies and young children are notorious for putting things in their mouths that do not belong and therefore have an increased risk of choking. If you find a sitter that you like who is not already certified, you can always offer to pay for her to take the class. You can check at your local Red Cross or community hospitals for a schedule of CPR courses.

When I had our first child, I had the grandparents take the course because I knew they would be sitting for us. We paid to have someone come to our house to teach the course, and then we had drinks and a wonderful supper afterwards. It was a great way for us all to get certified, and it also turned out to be a fun time.

When you are interviewing potential sitters, make it very clear of what your expectations are. It always helps to cover everything upfront so there are no surprises. If you need her to help out in the kitchen or with the laundry when the baby is asleep, now is the time to talk about it.

Do not feel like you have to make a decision at the time of the interview. It is best if you can meet with several people and pick the person who seems to be the best match. If you like two of the applicants, then try them both out and see who works out the best. You can always spread out the hours between the two sitters. It is good to have several people who can sit for you so you have a back up when you need one.

Breaking in a new sitter

Once you find someone who will sit for you, whether it is a person you previously knew or someone you hired from an ad, schedule a time for her to sit with your children while you are at the house. Allow at least 30 minutes or more to familiarize her with your home and make her aware of where everything is located, from the first-aid kit to the fire extinguishers. Show her where you keep your list of emergency and important phone numbers. It is also helpful to write down some general information about where your home is located, such as the closest crossroads, the name of your neighborhood, etc. What may seem to be extra detail now can be of great importance during an emergency when people are more likely to forget even the most basic information. Keep this emergency information posted in an obvious place so she can easily find it if needed.

You also want her to know what your rules are for your children so she can help to reinforce them. Being there the first time she sits makes you available for her to ask you any questions that may arise concerning your children or your home. It also allows you to see how well she gets along with your children. You do not want to make her feel awkward by hovering over her and your children, so try to stay out of sight but within earshot.

How to keep a sitter

Once you find a good sitter for your children, treat her well! Having a person that you trust watching children is a very big deal and does not happen every day, so you want to make sure she sticks around. Ask her what her favorite drinks and snacks are so you have something she likes when she is at your house. (College students love this, since most are always on a tight budget and appreciate anything they can get.) Little things like rounding up when paying her, remembering her at holidays or on her birthday, and asking her about her life show how much you care and that you appreciate her as a person.

It is also very important that your children respect the sitter and behave as they are supposed to. You will make your baby-sitter's job a lot easier and less frustrating if you support her by ensuring your children follow the rules. Have open communication with her about how your children behave when you are not there. A lot of times, younger sitters are uncomfortable with bringing up poor behavior, and it helps them if you ask specifically about how your children are doing.

If you help make your babysitter's job more enjoyable, it will be better for her, and most importantly, better for your children. This person is helping to take care of your children when you are not around, and if you have found a great caregiver, you should do what you can to keep her.

How to balance volunteer work

Whether you are a stay-at-home-mom or work outside the home, someone is always going to want you to volunteer to help out, be it at school, on your children's team, or at a church or other religious institution. Volunteering is a part of life, and at some point we all need to pitch in to help keep things going. The key is to know how to balance when you can help out and when you need to say "no."

Once it becomes known by a group, school, team, or organization that you are willing to volunteer, you can get caught in a vicious cycle that is hard to get out of and find yourself overcommitted. When everyone knows that you will volunteer, they tend to ask you more and more, and the more you say "yes," the more they ask you to do because they know you will say "yes" again. If you cannot say "no" when asked to help out, it is easy to find yourself spread too thin and become overwhelmed with your responsibilities and all that you have to do in addition to the normal busyness of your family's schedule.

There are three types of people when it comes to volunteering: 1. People who cannot say "no," 2. People who cannot say "yes," and 3. People who have learned to keep a balance between how much volunteer work they commit to and their responsibilities to their family. No matter which group you fall into, the tips below will help you learn to volunteer without over committing yourself.

▶ **Know and accept the constraints that you have to work around.** For example, if you have very young children at home with you when others are trying to recruit you to chaperone your older child's fieldtrip, accept the fact that it is just not going to happen. If you are like I was, getting a sitter just to make an important doctor's appointment was a big deal, so I accepted the fact that I could not chaperone fieldtrips. I did not have unlimited access to babysitters and knew that this just was not a good way for me to help out. Let people know upfront what your limitations are, and they will understand. Do not try to force something to work if it creates too much of burden on you and your family.

▶ **Know your strengths and what you are able to give.** If

you work all day and cannot attend your children's parties at school but love to cook, why not sign up to send in some of the food? Things that can be done after the children are in bed can be of great help to someone and still work into your schedule. If you are an outgoing person and do not mind calling people or even sending emails out to coordinate something, then volunteer to do that. Let it be known to people what you are able to do and ask how that might fit into their volunteer needs.

▶ **Spread out your commitments.** If you have several children, it is important to balance out how much you volunteer for each child. At the open house in the beginning of the year, take your day planner with you, and when they pull out the volunteer sheets, be strategic in what you sign up for. If you know that you are having your family at your house for Christmas as well as out-of-town guests, by all means do not sign up to help out with the Christmas party. Sign up for the Halloween or end-of-the-year party if that better fits your schedule. Immediately write on your calendar what you have committed to so that there are no surprises right before an event. Spread out what you sign up for so that it is balanced throughout the year. You have to be smart and thoughtful so your commitments do not get out of hand and make you and your family suffer.

▶ **When asked to help out on a big project, ask to sleep on it.** When approached by someone to take on a large task, tell him that you need to look at your calendar and think about it overnight. Ask if you can get back to him tomorrow to let him know. Always, always do this! There is nothing worse than agreeing to do something when you are caught up in the moment just to regret it later, or worse yet, have to tell someone that you changed your mind and cannot do it. Give the decision the thought time that it deserves. I always tell people—and it is very true—that I need to think about my answer because I do not want to commit to something to which I cannot give my all. Your decision will always be a better one if you think about it overnight.

➤ **Learn how to delegate.** Just because you have signed up to be in charge of an event does not mean that you have to do everything or even most of it. Ask others to help out to make the event a success. If you can find a handful of people to each do a little work, it will all add up and take the weight off you. Have a game plan for what you need done and make it clear to people what you are looking for. This makes it easier for them to help out, which ultimately means you will have more help and the event will be an even bigger success.

➤ **Learn to say "no."** It sounds so easy, but sometimes that one-syllable word can be difficult to say. If you cannot get the word "no" out when asked to commit to something, you cannot do, try "I just can't commit to that right now with all of my other responsibilities." If you are asked to volunteer for the whole week of a Vacation Bible School and know it is impossible due to your schedule, you could answer with, "I am not able to commit to that much time but I would be happy to help out the first morning of registration" or "I am unable to commit, but can I send in food for the volunteers or materials for the crafts?" Tell them if you cannot commit to the thing they are asking of you, but then let them know in what ways you are able to help out. There is always something that you can do to contribute.

This point should help out those people who cannot say

"yes." There is always something you can do, no matter how small. We all must pitch in to make things operate. You do not have to help out with everything all of the time, but even if your schedule is slammed packed, there is usually some way you can contribute once in a while, even if it seems minor.

When Mom gets sick

There are few words that can make a family shudder more than when they hear mom say, "I think I'm getting sick." A look of fear can be seen on each family member's face, because they all know what this means. A home that runs like a well-oiled machine can quickly turn to chaos if intentional thought is not given to when mom is out of commission.

The entire family needs to rise to the occasion and help out (where age appropriate). If you have taught your children to pitch in already, you will reap the rewards even more while you are ill in bed. Some kids take great pride in helping out when mom is sick because they see it as a way to help her to feel better. This is a good thing and definitely works to your advantage.

If you are just suffering from a cold or any other minor ailment, the effect on your family will only be slight and can be managed. However, for those illnesses that knock you out for several days or more, an organized approach to house management becomes necessary. Follow these tips to help keep your family and house in order and help you to recover quickly.

➤ **Do not try to be "supermom"!** If you try to keep doing the things that you normally do, you will wear yourself out and delay your recovery. When you are sick, you need to focus on the priorities, the first being that you recover quickly and completely, and let some things go.

➤ **Make a list of what is most important.** If you become very ill or are recovering from a surgery, you will want to have a list of what needs to be done for your spouse to refer to. Let him know exactly what he needs to do to keep the house together, from signing the kids' papers to packing lunches and doing the laundry. Also, write out where each child is supposed to be at what time. Things that you normally do by instinct can be overwhelming for your spouse. Having a detailed itinerary is very helpful and ensures everyone is where they are supposed to be. If the important tasks are written down, it is much easier for your family to remember everything and ensures that they are accomplished. This will give you a peace of mind in knowing that all is going well while you recover.

➤ **Take advantage of take-out food.** Having food delivered or picked up for supper will make dinner time much easier.

➤ **Get extra help from babysitters or other family members who live close by.** Babysitters are not just for date night. Call on people who can keep your children while you rest. They can even help out by running to the store, picking up your kids from school, helping your children with their homework, and running other errands you need accomplished.

➤ **Make use of disposable products.** Let your family utilize paper plates and cups to help keep cleanup at a minimum.

➤ **Do one small task each time you get out of bed.** As you regain some energy, try to do one little thing each time you get up to get something to drink or to use the restroom. Even if it is just switching out the wash or loading the top rack of the dishwasher, these small tasks will help out. Do not overdue it, but if you have the energy to accomplish one thing to help keep the house together, try to do it.

➤ **Make sure the house stays germ-free.** Make sure the rest of your family does not get your illness by having them sanitize door knobs, bathrooms, phones, and kitchen surfaces, including the handles to appliances and sinks. Also use the high temperature setting on your dishwasher to make sure everything is sanitized. Have everyone be diligent about taking their vitamins and getting plenty of Vitamin C. You want to ensure your illness does not make its way through your entire family.

➤ **Get plenty of rest and fluids.** Even as you are feeling better, make sure you take it easy. The demands of being a parent are great, and you do not want to have a relapse.

➤ **Take advantage of your down time.** When you feel up to it, use the time you need in bed to read some of the magazines you never find time to get to or go through a cookbook to pick out new recipes. It can also be a great time to catch up on your children's baby books or scrapbooking.

➤ **Enjoy your family realizing exactly how much you really do!** Your family will get along just fine while you are out of commission, and it will do everyone some good to appreciate all of the hard work you put into keeping the family running.

Simple steps towards a happier You

To help you recharge and keep up the attitude and energy that is needed for parenting, you must make the decision to make time for yourself. Even the little things that you can do to take care of yourself can add up to making you feel like you are not just a nurse, chauffeur, cook, maid, and referee. I have discovered some tricks that help me to recharge and allow me to take better care of myself, even with the demands of raising four young boys. I used to think that I needed large chunks of time to take care of me, but I soon came to realize that moments stolen here and there could also help make a difference.

➤ **Maintain a healthy diet.** We all know that we feel better when we eat better. It is easy to neglect your diet when you are wrapped up in everyone else's needs but you have to make it a priority. It is proven that a healthy diet gives you more energy and you stay healthier. Keep healthy snacks, such as mixed nuts or granola bars, and water bottles in your car so you have something to munch on when you are driving everyone where they need to be. This helps curb you appetite, which can prevent the urge for you to grab something that is not healthy when you get too hungry.

➤ **Get plenty of rest.** This can be a hard one, but make yourself get the rest you need. You will never be able to catch up on everything, so stop trying. Set goals for your day that are realistic and stop there. You will be more productive and in a much better mood the next day if you get the rest you need.

➤ **Choose one morning a week to sleep in.** During the week, I am always the first one up, but come Saturday, I put on my sleep mask and everyone knows that it's mom's day to sleep in. Let your spouse feed the kids and keep peace in the house while you get your needed rest. If you are a single parent with older children, put together a deal that gives them an incentive to let you sleep in. Do not forget to pull down the shades or put on a sleep mask so you will be able to sleep a little bit longer than you are used to.

➤ **Get in the shower.** With young children, this necessary part of life can start to feel like a luxury. If you have an infant, place him in an infant carrier in the bathroom with you while you shower. Using a clear shower curtain or shower door allows you to see your baby while you bathe. Most babies will fall asleep at the sound of the running water, so you can time it around his nap. For older babies and toddlers, you can set them up in your bathroom with some toys and books so they can happily play and you know they are safe while you sneak in a shower. Getting cleaned up and putting on some fresh clothes can make you feel like a new person. After a hectic day with the kids, don't forget about this simple way to feel rejuvenated.

(If your spouse can watch the children while you sneak in a bubble bath, that's even better!)

➤ **Use a body moisturizer.** Before you even get out of the shower, apply a full body lotion to lock in moisture. I found that as soon as I stepped out of the shower I was free game for my children, but as long as I was behind that shower curtain they knew I was off limits. This made me start putting on lotion before I got out and I found it made my skin even softer because I was still partially wet; this helps to lock in the moisture. Try applying a body lotion or spray that contains lavender for your evening showers to help you relax.

➤ **Keep an extra stash of facial cleaner and moisturizer in your child's bathroom.** Washing your face at the end of the day and applying a good moisturizer is important to protect your skin and keep it looking younger longer. At the end of crazy day with the children, you may sometimes want to just fall into the bed without taking the time to take care of your face properly. To prevent this, keep an extra set of facial products in your child's bathroom so you can easily wash and moisturize your face while your child is bathing. (This is assuming, of course, that your child can safely bathe unassisted.)

➤ **Wear sunscreen every day.** We all know that sun damage is not only unhealthy, but it speeds up the aging process. Once you have children, you will probably be spending more time outdoors and need to protect your skin more than you may have in the past. Even if you are going about a normal day and will not be spending an extended about of time in the sun, it is still important to apply at least a sunscreen of SPF 35. If you protect your skin now, you will be very thankful later.

➤ **Keep a nail file and hand moisturizer in your car.** Nails are easily neglected and usually take a lot of abuse when you are raising kids. Constantly washing your hands is healthy but wreaks havoc on your nails and hands. When you have a few minutes in the car, for example, if you are in line or at a bank drive-thru, use this time to file your nails and apply a good moisturizer. Don't forget about cuticle cream, which can work wonders too.

➤ **Paint your nails before you pull out of the driveway.** When do moms ever stay still enough to paint their nails and not have them get smudged? For me, it was only in the car driving my kids here and there. Even if you do not like color on your nails, a clear protective coat is important to protect and strengthen them. After you and your children are buckled in the car, apply a coat of polish to your nails before you put the car in drive. The time it takes you to get where you are going should be enough time for your nails to dry. If your drive will be short, try holding your hands out the window or in front of the AC vents to speed up the drying process.

➤ **Sneak in a little exercise throughout the day.** If you simply cannot find the time to complete a full workout session, the little things you do throughout the day can add up to a lot. Listed are a few examples of how you can fit in some exercise into even the busiest of schedules:

> ➤ While a child is bathing, age appropriate of course, you can do sit-ups or push-ups.
> ➤ When your child is in the crib, hold onto the side and play peek-a-boo while doing deep-knee-bends.
> ➤ When you are outside playing with your children, work in some walking lunges or jumping-jacks.
> ➤ Try out an exercise video that your child can participate in with you.
> ➤ Purchase some dumbbells for yourself and one-pound weights for your child and make up a work out together.
> ➤ Do stretches with your child. Increasing your flexibility is very helpful to your body, and your child will enjoy doing it with you if you make it fun.
> ➤ When cleaning up the house, view each trip up the stairs

as an opportunity to get in a leg workout. Instead of getting frustrated by the many trips you need to make up and down the stairs, think of it as a workout and enjoy what it is doing for your legs.

➤ Play tag with your children to get your heart pumping.

➤ While talking on the phone, keep some dumbbells handy and alternate arms doing bicep curls, overhead arm extensions (to work your triceps), or overhead presses. You could also try calf raises on your steps to help tone your legs.

➤ While working on your computer, you can get in a few sets of the arm exercises mentioned above.

➤ If you watch TV anytime during the day, make the most of it by turning this into your exercise time. You can get in a good workout whether utilizing a tread mill, dumbbells, resistance bands, or just the furniture in your home.

Anything that you can squeeze in will make you feel better about yourself, improve your health, and tone your body. It may also encourage you to do a little more the next time, and then before you know it you have established a good workout routine.

➤ **Put something cool on your eyes**. Putting cool slices of cucumbers, chilled tea bags, or a refrigerated gel eye mask can work wonders for you after a sleepless night with one of your children. It reduces puffiness and helps you to wake up feeling a little more refreshed.

➤ **Read a fashion or decorating magazine**. Just reading up-to-date periodicals can make you feel more in touch with the world. Parenting magazines are very informative and great to read, but also allow time to read about other things too. Grab a magazine to read while you are watching your children happily play in the bath tub. (Again, only if they can bathe safely without a constant eye on them.) Just keeping current on what is in vogue helps you to feel like you are up with the world.

➤ **Establish a date night.** Make it a priority to schedule some time for just you and your spouse. Even though you have time with him after the children are in bed, it is not the same as going out somewhere to be together. When you go out, you can leave all of your responsibilities at home, allowing the two of you to relax and reconnect.

➤ **Schedule a date with your girlfriends.** It is healthy and rejuvenating to get together with some friends who can serve as a support group. Just reliving the good ole' days with high school or college friends can help remind you that there is more to you than just a being a mom and wife. Also, sharing some of your thoughts and concerns with others who are going through what you are can be comforting and insightful.

➤ **Make time for your family to help those less fortunate.** You will quickly count your blessings and appreciate all that you have been given, if you make an effort to help those in need. We all need to be reminded that we should give back to our community. In a World that lives in excess, it is a healthy reminder to you and your children to recognize that there are a lot of people who are without the basic needs in life. There are many different ways that your family can give back to your community. It is a great way for a family to work together to help out others in need. Check out the local charities in your area and find one that your family feels called to become involved.

➤ **Stay organized!** This is actually a way of taking care of yourself because you will not be as stressed and your life will run more smoothly. This allows you to be a happier and healthier person. We all dreamed about having a family and being a great parent, but most of the time it is not as easy as we envisioned. By just staying organized, you will be able to better enjoy your life and the wonderful family that you have been blessed with!

To order copies of

Managing Life with Kids

or to learn more tips on how to
improve your life and family

please visit

todaysultimate**mom**.com

Made in the USA